MASTERPIECES

BLACK CAT

Written by Rob Mason

A TWOCAN PUBLICATION

©2016. Published by twocan under licence from Sunderland AFC.

ISBN 978-1-911502-21-0

PICTURE CREDITS: Getty Images, Action Images, Mirrorpix, Press Association, Sunderland AFC.

Outside the north-east, many people remain amazed that Sunderland still regularly pull in 40,000 crowds, when only supporters pushing 60 can remember the club winning its solitary major post-war trophy.

Of course, if you grow up on Wearside and throughout County Durham you are raised with red and white folklore, tales of the time when Sunderland had won the league more than anyone else, when the Lads were the only club to have never played outside the top flight.

Sunderland are still one of the country's biggest clubs in the eyes of those who follow them. The Black Cats may not have ever played in the Champions League and struggle to make an impression in the Premier League, but with their rich history, loyal fan-base and the biggest and best stadium built in the country in the second half of the twentieth century, Sunderland are still a force to be reckoned with.

This book of 50 of Sunderland's greatest players aims to celebrate some of the most naturally talented men supporters have had the pleasure of watching. Fans long for a side to compare with Stokoe's Stars, the greats of the thirties and the dim distant past when Sunderland were champions five times in 21 years.

In Masterpieces, modern day players such as Defoe, Kirchhoff, Khazri and Ndong stand side by side with heroes of the great days at the Stadium of Light, including Quinny and SuperKev, as well as Magic Johnston and Summerbee who supplied them, and of course Juliooo, whose talent was sublime.

From the closing decades at Roker Park there is the 'Son of Pele', alongside the likes of Marco, Arnott and Rowell, as well as heroes from the Team of '73, 'The Bank of England' side and some of the greatest pre-war players you may have heard of, but perhaps not know too much about.

Sunderland can get under the skin of players, it can become almost a tattoo, an indelible image that lasts a lifetime. For supporters that lifetime 'tattoo' is one that hopefully filters out the dark periods and focusses on the brighter times, so here we shine a light on the most magical masterpieces there are to enjoy.

Stan Anderson is a giant of north-east football. He captained Sunderland, Newcastle and Middlesbrough, but despite leading the Magpies to promotion as captain in 1965 and managing Middlesbrough to promotion in 1967, it is his boyhood team Sunderland with which he is synonymous.

402 of his 504 league appearances were with Sunderland, his overall total of 447 being surpassed only by Len Ashurst amongst outfield players.

He was the local youngster good enough to more than hold his own amongst the stellar talents of 'The Bank of England Team' in the fifties and during the sixties he was the only Sunderland player to be capped at full level by England.

A maestro of a wing-half in an era of great wing-halves, Stan surely should have been capped more than twice. However in an era where sending offs were a rarity, a dismissal against Bulgaria at Under-23 level in 1957 did him no favours with the blazers. Stan had captained his country at schoolboy level and won a cap at 'B' level.

The match of his life was an FA Cup third round tie against Arsenal watched by just under 60,000 at Roker in 1961 when he scored twice, including a rare header, to help Sunderland come from behind to win 2-1.

ANDERSON

The emergence of Martin Harvey led to his shock transfer to Newcastle two years later, but Stan returned to Wearside for a richly deserved testimonial. Having signed for all-time great Raich Carter when he joined 'Boro, Stan's connections with Sunderland continued through the decades with the appointments of Peter Reid and Sam Allardyce who Anderson coached as young players at Bolton.

FULL NAME:
Stan Anderson

POSITION:
Right-half

DATE OF BIRTH:
27 February 1934

PLACE OF BIRTH:
Horden

SUNDERLAND DEBUT:
Sunderland 1-1 Portsmouth
4 October 1952

APPEARANCES:
447

GOALS:
35

By definition only the finest artists produce masterpieces. In Julio Arca Sunderland had a player who could cover a canvas with precision.

Arca mixed artistry with application. His talent provided supporters with many memorable moments but Julio was never the type to produce one minute of magic and spend the other 89 minutes admiring it, his work-rate was as impressive as his creativity.

Arca's defining goal in a Sunderland shirt illustrated this combination of class and commitment. It was at Bradford City in August 2003 when Julio broke from box to box before applying a finish that had the touch of a master. Despite the energy expended in breaking from one end to the other, Julio had the composure to decide to chip the 'keeper and the ability to produce a magical touch deft enough to lift the ball exquisitely over the 6'5" goalie.

It had been at Fulham's Craven Cottage, playing against England U21s for Argentina U21's that the teenage Arca produced a performance that persuaded Sunderland manager Peter Reid to invest a reported £3.5m to bring the youngster not only across the Atlantic but from the southern to the northern hemisphere in the first summer of the new millennium. It was a massive move for such a young player, and not simply in football terms, but Arca adapted quickly.

ARCA

A debut goal against West Ham helped but over and above that the crowd took to Julio because they could see instantly that he had a touch of class and that he was putting his heart and soul into every game.

Spanish speaking Julio was helped by Portuguese speaking Brazilian teammate Emerson Thome. That undoubtedly helped Julio settle but he always looked at home and at ease on the pitch.

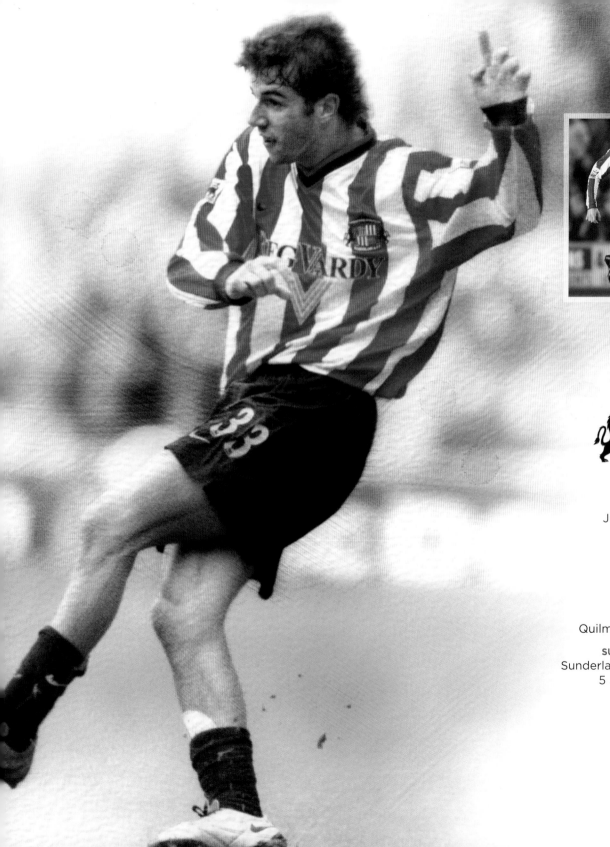

FULL NAME:
Julio Andres Arca

POSITION:
Left-midfield

DATE OF BIRTH:
31 January 1981

PLACE OF BIRTH:
Quilmes Bernal, Argentina

SUNDERLAND DEBUT:
Sunderland 1-1 West Ham United
5 September 2000

APPEARANCES:
165 (12)

GOALS:
23

FULL NAME:
Julio Andres Arca

POSITION:
Left-midfield

DATE OF BIRTH:
31 January 1981

PLACE OF BIRTH:
Quilmes Bernal, Argentina

SUNDERLAND DEBUT:
Sunderland 1-1 West Ham United
5 September 2000

APPEARANCES:
165 (12)

GOALS:
23

In the maelstrom of midfield in the fastest league in the world, the boy from Buenos Aires always looked like he had that bit more time on the ball than those buzzing around him.

What gave Julio that extra moment in possession was often the adhesive first touch that killed it stone dead at his feet. A left-back before he arrived in England, having coped with the geographical move that took him from four figure crowds with his first club Argentinos Juniors to 40,000 plus gates on Wearside, being asked to play in an unfamiliar midfield berth was just one more thing Julio made look easy.

Sunderland finished seventh in the Premier League in Arca's first year, struggled to just stay up a season later and were dismally demoted a further 12 months on, with Julio largely a bystander due to injury. Staying at Sunderland at a time when many of his colleagues left, Julio was Player of the Year as he helped the Lads to the semi-finals of the FA Cup and Play-Offs before contributing a goal per four games as Sunderland lifted the Championship in 2005.

The following season sadly would be Julio's last for Sunderland as relegation was suffered again, Arca missing more than a third of the campaign. His final goal was a sublime free kick in a win at Middlesbrough who would be his next club. In fact Julio would play more for Boro than he did for Sunderland,

JULIO

ARCA

but it would be Sunderland with whom he remained synonymous and truly loved. Refusing to celebrate when he later scored against the Wearsiders, Julio later maintained a home in Sunderland, returned to prove his love of the game for playing for Hylton Road pub The Willow Pond and went on to reprise the magic with South Shields while coaching back at the SAFC Academy.

Kevin Arnott was certainly a masterpiece. He hit the heights when at his best with Sunderland, but given his talent, the other clubs on his CV should have been stellar names.

Kevin was Sunderland's answer to Glenn Hoddle. He had all vision to see the game like a war leader in a control room. His radar could be finely tuned and his ability to strike was rapier like.

Although a pupil at St. Aidan's in Sunderland, Kevin came from a black and white family and reserved two of his finest moments for derby matches. When Jermain Defoe thumped home a sensational winner against Newcastle in 2015, the question on everyone's lips was 'When had there last been a better derby goal?' The answer was Arnott's magnificent floated chip over Magpies 'keeper Mick Mahoney at the Roker End on Good Friday 1977. If you want a masterpiece of a goal, that was it.

Although he also scored on the night promotion was won against West Ham in 1980, Arnott was always more of a maker than a taker of goals. Known as one of 'Charlie's Angels' when brought into the team as one of chief scout Charlie Ferguson's protégé's alongside Shaun Elliott and Gary Rowell, the trio had progressed together. On the day of Rowell's legendary hat-trick at St. James' in 1979, the pick of the goals was the second, of which Rowell recalled,

ARNOTT

"Kevin Arnott picked me out with a great through ball. I'd played with Kev for years and years - we played together as kids, so we had a good understanding of each other's game. I'd make runs and he'd pick me out. So Kev put it right in front of me. 2-0 up. Brilliant."

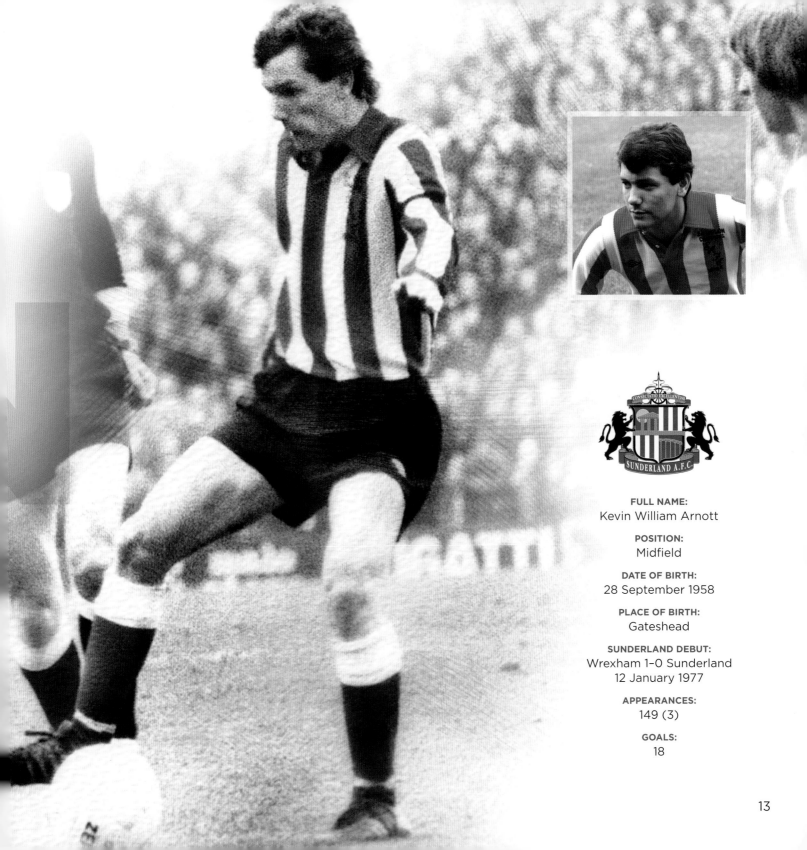

FULL NAME:
Kevin William Arnott

POSITION:
Midfield

DATE OF BIRTH:
28 September 1958

PLACE OF BIRTH:
Gateshead

SUNDERLAND DEBUT:
Wrexham 1–0 Sunderland
12 January 1977

APPEARANCES:
149 (3)

GOALS:
18

FULL NAME:
Leonard Ashurst

POSITION:
Left-back

DATE OF BIRTH:
10 March 1939

PLACE OF BIRTH:
Liverpool

SUNDERLAND DEBUT:
Sunderland 0-2 Ipswich Town
20 September 1958

APPEARANCES:
452 (6)

GOALS:
4

No one has played as many games for Sunderland as an outfield player than Len Ashurst. Only goalkeeper Jim Montgomery surpasses Len's total of 458 games, a tally he proudly adds to his autograph.

One of a trio of youngsters who went on to wrack up over 1100 appearances between them when they were simultaneously handed debuts one autumnal day in Sunderland's inaugural second-tier season in 1958, Ashurst went on to make the number three shirt his own. An ever-present in the club's first promotion campaign, Len made at least 40 appearances in every season between 1960/61 and 1965/66

Nick-named 'Lennie the Lion', other than the moniker itself, Len had nothing in common with the popular children's entertainer of the time, Terry Hall. Equally, the likening to children's TV favourites 'Bill & Ben' had no founding other than the theme tune where the ditty associating him with his fellow full-back Cecil Irwin went along the lines of 'Cec & Len, Cec & Len, flower pot men..." Far from being a soft touch likely to be part of children's entertainment 'Lennie the Lion' was a tough full-back in an age when wingers often had good reason not to relish their immediate opponent.

In Len's day, being able to defend was the essential criteria for being a full-back compared to the modern game where sometimes full-backs' attacking attributes are often seen as

ASHURST

almost as important as their ability to help protect their own goal. Nonetheless, Len was no slouch when it came to lending his weight to the attack. A hard working player who got forward in support of his front men when he could, Ashurst got his name on the score-sheet four times, most notably with a thunderbolt against Newcastle United in 1963.

FULL NAME:
Leonard Ashurst

POSITION:
Left-back

DATE OF BIRTH:
10 March 1939

PLACE OF BIRTH:
Liverpool

SUNDERLAND DEBUT:
Sunderland 0-2 Ipswich Town
20 September 1958

APPEARANCES:
452 (6)

GOALS:
4

Never happier than when he had Jim McNab and George Mulhall making up the left flank in front of him, Len wasn't so impressed when Jim Baxter took McNab's place at left half and left Len one on one with his winger.

Moreover the mid-sixties; which saw some key members of the '64 promotion team being side-lined in favour of new faces Len perceived to be disruptive influences at the club he'd grown to love, left him exasperated at times.

Twenty years after being a promotion winner Len had another opportunity to stamp his authority on the club when he returned as manager. His managerial reign began brightly. The team were seventh in the top flight in early November following back to back 3-0 home wins with only the second post-war cup run to Wembley under way.

Unfortunately things unravelled for Len as the League Cup final was lost due to an own goal and a missed penalty. With league form tailing away and collapsing after the cup final Len's team went down, with the club legend being dismissed by chairman Tom Cowie in 1985.

The stories behind Ashurst's total of 524 games at Sunderland as player or manager were fully covered in his candid self-penned autobiography 'Left Back in Time', published in the week of his 70th birthday in 2009.

LEN ASHURST

Len's standing in the game saw him employed by the Premier League to help oversee the development of academy football. He also was recognised by the League Managers' Association having achieved the rare feat of managing in 1,000 senior matches. After six decades in the game, Len retired from his final role as a Premier League Match Delegate, assessing referees, at the close of the 2015/16 season.

FULL NAME:
Jim Curran Baxter

POSITION:
Left-half

DATE OF BIRTH:
29 September 1939

PLACE OF BIRTH:
Hill of Beath, Fife, Scotland

SUNDERLAND DEBUT:
Leeds 1-0 Sunderland
21 August 1965

APPEARANCES:
98

GOALS:
12

In any assessment of Sunderland's greatest players Jim Baxter simply has to be included. In fact, he would make the top 100 of the United Kingdom's greatest players. How high Baxter would rank would depend upon whether judgement was based on sheer ability or the maximising of that talent.

In terms of pure ability 'Slim Jim' ranks with the very best. In terms of maximising his natural gifts 'Bacardi Jim' joins the list of footballers who failed to extract every last drop of their potential.

Baxter was a brilliant player. Of that there is no doubt. His left foot was known as 'the claw'. Teammate Bruce Stuckey remembered, 'Jim would just tell me to run and when I got there the ball would be waiting for me, and it would be.'

In the pantheon of Sunderland's players probably only the Clown Price of Soccer, Len Shackleton, could make the ball 'talk' in the way that Baxter could.

Famously at Wembley in 1967 when Scotland became the first team to defeat England when they were world champions, it was Baxter who stole the show, impudently doing keepy-uppies in the centre circle.

BAXTER

Baxter was on Sunderland's books at the time. Earlier in the year; on the first occasion I saw a first team match, Baxter took a penalty at the Roker End.

It was a fourth round FA Cup tie where Sunderland beat Peterborough United 7-1. Already 6-1 up, as Baxter stood up after placing the ball he pointed to the goalkeeper to show where he was going to place his shot. Sure enough Slim Jim stroked the ball to exactly where he said it would go.

As goalkeeper Tony Millington forlornly looked back after diving the wrong way, Baxter made eye contact with him and shrugged his shoulders as if to say 'I gave you a chance.' Even as an eight-year-old, that told me Baxter was different.

Unfortunately, that difference was also his undoing. In late life a licensee who passed away at the age of 61, Jim suffered serious ill health due to his love of alcohol. Not one to look after himself physically, the 'Slim Jim' moniker he arrived with after winning ten trophies with Rangers gradually became replaced with the nickname 'Bacardi Jim', not least as he lost any claim to be slim. His game wasn't about pace though, he always let the ball, and his teammates, do the work.

His lack of professionalism did not sit well with his long established teammates schooled under the disciplinarian manager Alan Brown, whereas Baxter was signed by his Scotland boss and Rangers legend Ian McColl who also signed Baxter's cousin George Kinnell.

BAXTER

A split arose in the dressing room with the maverick Baxter, alas a sparkling individual who didn't fit into a team framework at Roker Park.

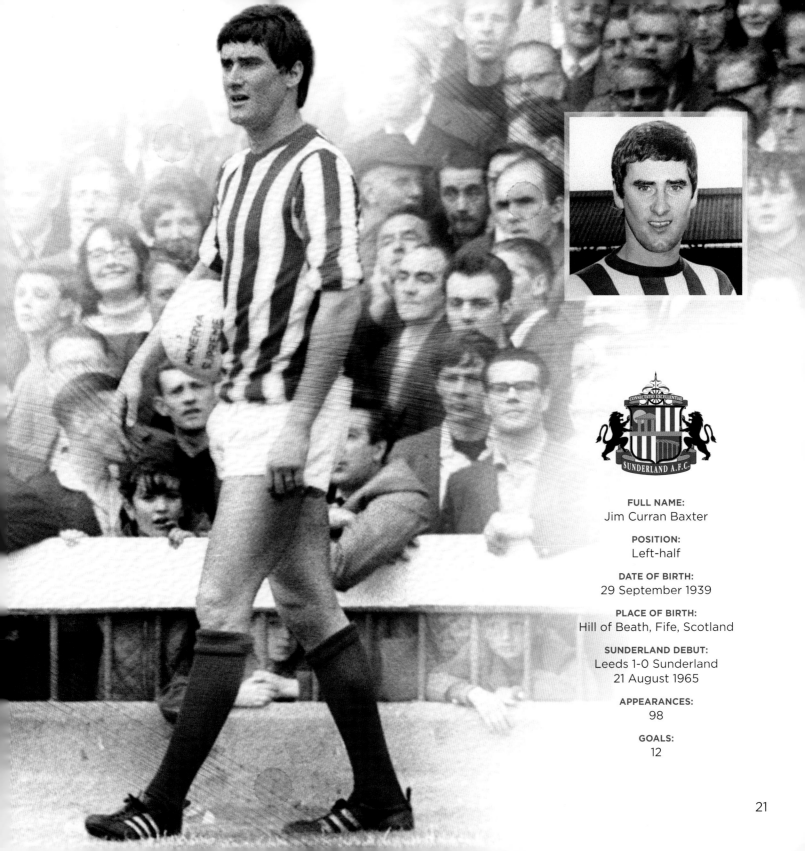

FULL NAME:
Jim Curran Baxter

POSITION:
Left-half

DATE OF BIRTH:
29 September 1939

PLACE OF BIRTH:
Hill of Beath, Fife, Scotland

SUNDERLAND DEBUT:
Leeds 1-0 Sunderland
21 August 1965

APPEARANCES:
98

GOALS:
12

Only four players have turned out more for the Lads than 'Benno', but when he was signed in 1984 his tribunal-set fee included a payment of £20,000 after 20 appearances, in addition to an initial transfer fee of £65,000.

There was little doubt Gary would play many more than 20 games as the man signing him knew exactly what he was getting. That manager was Len Ashurst who had managed Gary at Cardiff City and who is one of only two outfield players to play more games for Sunderland than Bennett.

Gary wasted no time in getting on the right side of the Wearside crowd, scoring after just two minutes of his debut against legendary England 'keeper Peter Shilton. That goal put Gary in the headlines that he would frequently hit. As a defender his priority was to prevent goals, but the Mancunian had a habit of finding the net at the other end in key games.

As a man whose first professional club was Manchester City, 'Benno' particularly enjoyed a spectacular last-minute winner against Manchester United at Roker Park in 1990. Think of Gazza's goal for England v Scotland at Euro '96 and Gary's effort was similar, only perhaps a bit better given the defender he lifted the ball over before curling his shot home was Britain's costliest defender at the time, Gary Pallister.

SAFC's Player of the Year in 1986/87 and 1993/94, Gary made his final appearance in red and white against Luton in April 1995.

BENNETT

After extending his career with Carlisle United, Scarborough and Darlington, Gary had a spell as Darlington's manager under the chairmanship of George Reynolds.

For the last decade 'Benno' has been the BBC summariser on Sunderland games for local radio and in 2016 took over as chairman of the Sunderland Former Players' Association.

FULL NAME:
Gary Ernest Bennett

POSITION:
Defender

DATE OF BIRTH:
4 December 1961

PLACE OF BIRTH:
Manchester

SUNDERLAND DEBUT:
Sunderland 3-1 Southampton
25 August 1984

APPEARANCES:
434 (9)

GOALS:
25

23

Captain of the last Sunderland team to contest the FA Cup final in 1992, Paul Bracewell was a top class midfielder who would have won far more than three England caps, if not for injury. Nonetheless, he won the league and European Cup Winners' Cup with Everton, for whom he also contested another three FA Cup finals.

Going into the 2016/17 season, 'Brace' was in his fifth spell at Sunderland, either as a player, coach or assistant manager. First brought to the club by manager Alan Durban who had given him his league debut at Stoke, Bracewell was a player with an excellent touch. He was a crisp passer of the ball and a player who if he misplaced a pass it was a shock. Bracewell believed in keeping the ball and as well as being skilled at delivering a pass, he was tremendous at receiving one.

Always on the move, Paul knew exactly where to be to give a teammate in possession an easy pass. He had the energy to do this from the first minute to the last and was invaluable as a man who knitted play together.

A Championship winner with Sunderland in 1996, he also won that trophy three years earlier with Newcastle while three years later he won Division two with Fulham who he went on to manage. He also managed Halifax Town and coached Walsall.

BRACEWEL

Despite not playing at all in 1986/87 and making only four cup appearances the following season while with Everton (after a bad injury sustained at Newcastle in a collision with one-time Sunderland forward Billy Whitehurst), Brace's tenacity meant he still managed a massive 719 career appearances of which 145 for Everton was the most he made for any club other than Sunderland.

FULL NAME:
Paul William Bracewell

POSITION:
Midfield

DATE OF BIRTH:
19 July 1962

PLACE OF BIRTH:
Heswall

SUNDERLAND DEBUT:
Sunderland 1-1 Norwich City
27 August 1983

APPEARANCES:
268 (2)

GOALS:
6

Sunderland's oldest living player in 2016, Ivor Broadis was player-manager of Carlisle United when he was just 23 – and transferred himself to Sunderland! The fee of £18,000 was a record both for Carlisle and the Third Division North.

Broadis was an imaginative attacking schemer who had a good shot on him and was never afraid to exploit it. He missed just one game in his first full season at Roker Park, but managed just 20 games in the following campaign, although he did average a goal every other match that year, a tally that included a Boxing Day hat-trick in a 5-3 victory away to Manchester United.

He was Manchester bound within a year, albeit to City, after just five games of the following season. Two years later he was back in the north-east with Newcastle before returning to Carlisle after under two seasons.

Broadis was also to have a spell just across the border with Queen of the South as well as making a guest appearance for Third Lanark. Retiring in 1960, Ivor moved into coaching and later journalism where his words were highly respected.

Capped by England 14 times, the last two appearances coming against Switzerland and Uruguay at the 1954 World Cup finals, Broadis also represented the Football League three times.

BROADIS

Ironically, it was through the Football League that he was known as Ivor. Christened Ivan, his name was mis-read on a contract and he was duly registered by the League as Ivor, a name that stuck with him for the rest of his days.

FULL NAME:
Ivan Arthur Broadis

POSITION:
Inside-right

DATE OF BIRTH:
18 December 1922

PLACE OF BIRTH:
Poplar, London

SUNDERLAND DEBUT:
Arsenal 5-0 Sunderland
5 February 1949

APPEARANCES:
84

GOALS:
27

FULL NAME:
Charles Murray Buchan

POSITION:
Inside-right/centre-forward

DATE OF BIRTH:
22 September 1891

PLACE OF BIRTH:
Plumstead, London

SUNDERLAND DEBUT:
Tottenham Hotspur 1-1 Sunderland
1 April 1911

APPEARANCES:
411

GOALS:
222

Sunderland's all-time top league goalscorer, Charlie Buchan was Sunderland's top scorer eight times and a huge figure in the sport both during and after his playing days.

A Londoner by birth, Buchan began locally and represented Arsenal (Woolwich Arsenal as they were then) as an amateur before coming to Sunderland from Leyton in 1910 for a fee of £1,250. At first he found it hard to settle. Rather like another ex-Arsenal forward signed eight-and-a-half decades later who became a hero after having to initially win over the crowd, Niall Quinn, Buchan was not an instant hero. Indeed at one point he returned home to London necessitating manager Bob Kyle to travel to the capital to convince him to return.

Kyle's advice was sound. Buchan became the star man of a Sunderland team that came so close to the 'double' before World War One and remained a leading side after the war.

Only Bobby Gurney exceeds Buchan's overall Sunderland goals tally with 228 to Buchan's 222, but in terms of league goals only Buchan's 209 is a record that will be almost impossible to beat in the modern game. Goodness knows how many Buchan and Gurney would have scored had they both not lost some of their best years to the world wars. During the Great War Buchan would win the Military Medal and serve with the Sherwood Foresters and the Grenadier Guards.

That Military Medal took its place alongside league title winner's and FA Cup runner's-up medals won with Sunderland in 1912/13.

BUCHAN

Charlie top scored with 27 league goals in 36 games as the league was won and added another half-a-dozen in nine cup appearances. That haul included five in a game against Liverpool as he became the first man to score as many in a league game for the club.

Despite the outbreak of war in 1914 football continued until the end of the 1914/15 season, Buchan scoring Sunderland's last goal before football stopped as he completed a hat-trick against Spurs.

Charlie would pick up where he left off by netting the club's first league goal after the war against Aston Villa four years later, the first of 27 league and cup goals he'd score that season. He'd net 27 just in the league the year after.

Consistently productive, there were 21 the following season before his haul of 30 (plus another in the cup) made him the country's top scorer in 1922/23, his goals helping the Lads to runners'-up spot.

Sunderland would finish a place lower a year later when Buchan's 25 goals were more than double that of the club's second top scorer with Charlie being England's centre-forward in their first-ever international at Wembley that year. He had scored in all but one of his five previous internationals, but his outing against Scotland under the then new twin towers would be his last for his country.

The following season, 1924/25 would be his final one on Wearside before Arsenal, undaunted by a player who would turn 34 less than a month into the new season, came in for him. They'd had a reminder of what Charlie could do as he scored his last goal at Roker Park against the Gunners.

Arsenal were only willing to pay half of the £4,000 fee demanded for the veteran, but legendary manager Herbert Chapman was determined to make Buchan his first signing and agreed to pay £2,000 plus £100 for every goal Charlie scored in his first season. Sunderland ended up with more than the fee they demanded as Buchan bagged 21 in his first Highbury campaign.

BUCHAN

After collecting another FA Cup runners'-up medal in 1927, Charlie hung up his shooting boots and moved into journalism. He became a famous voice as well as a famous face as he commentated on England games in the early years of radio before his 'Charlie Buchan's Football Monthly' became the top selling football magazine in the world. Buchan came up with the idea of the Footballer of the Year award. Had it existed in his playing days no doubt he'd have been a winner.

FULL NAME:
Charles Murray Buchan

POSITION:
Inside-right/centre-forward

DATE OF BIRTH:
22 September 1891

PLACE OF BIRTH:
Plumstead, London

SUNDERLAND DEBUT:
Tottenham Hotspur 1-1 Sunderland
1 April 1911

APPEARANCES:
411

GOALS:
222

FULL NAME:
John Middleton Campbell

POSITION:
Centre-forward

DATE OF BIRTH:
19 February 1870

PLACE OF BIRTH:
Renton

SUNDERLAND DEBUT:
Blackburn Rovers 4-2 Sunderland
18 January 1890

APPEARANCES:
215

GOALS:
154

Only Davie Halliday and Brian Clough better Johnny Campbell's ratio of goals to games for Sunderland, Campbell's 154 goals from only 215 games giving him a ratio of 0.716 goals per game.

To put it into context, Campbell played 20 games fewer than SuperKev, but scored 24 more goals than the modern-day hero Phillips.

Campbell was the first man to be top scorer in the top flight two years running. He was the battering ram centre-forward of 'The Team of All The Talents' who won the league title in 1892, 1893 and 1895. In Sunderland's first title-winning year, Johnny bagged 32 goals which is all the more impressive when you realise they only played 30 games - and even better when you note that Campbell only played in 24 of them! Twice that season he scored four goals in a game, the second occasion being on the day the championship was secured. In the same season he scored another seven goals in FA Cup appearances as the Lads reached the semi-final.

A year later he top-scored again with 30 goals in 27 games plus a goal a game in three cup ties. Runners'-up in 1894 when Campbell collected 18 goals in 25 appearances, the title was lifted again a year later, this time Johnny playing all 30 games, scoring 21 times. Astonishingly, he failed to register in Sunderland's record 11-1 victory the same season in the cup, although he did bag two in the next round.

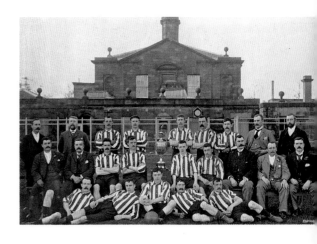

CAMPBELL

While he didn't win the cup with Sunderland, he did win the Scottish Cup with Renton. His half-brother Robert Campbell became Sunderland's manager for Johnny's last season when the goals dried up as he scored just four times in 35 games in all competitions. Sadly Johnny Campbell died in poverty aged just 36.

FULL NAME:
Horatio Stratton Carter

POSITION:
Inside-forward

DATE OF BIRTH:
21 December 1913

PLACE OF BIRTH:
Sunderland

SUNDERLAND DEBUT:
Sheffield Wednesday 3-1 Sunderland
15 October 1932

APPEARANCES:
278

GOALS:
128

Raich Carter was arguably the finest footballer ever to play for Sunderland. Granted, 'King' Charlie Hurley won the Player of the Century award in 1979. However, that poll came a decade after Hurley departed, whereas there weren't too many people around who had seen Carter's final Sunderland match 40 years earlier.

Shack of course must have a claim to the accolade, as might Charlie Buchan or from even earlier Jimmy Millar or Ted Doig. They each won four championship medals at Sunderland as part of the Team of All The Talents, but Carter's claim to be Sunderland's best-ever player stands up to scrutiny.

In an all-time England team, many would include Carter at inside forward, such is his renown in the national game. Tommy Lawton, one of England's great centre-forwards remarked, "He would be there for me in any team of immortals. I know of no other man who measured up so well as the complete footballer."

Carter captained his home-town team to their first-ever FA Cup triumph in 1937, scoring the decisive second goal in a 3-1 victory. Raich had been married a few days previously and as he received the cup from the Queen, she remarked, 'That's a nice wedding present for you.' Carter's Best Man had been centre-forward Bobby Gurney. A year earlier the pair had netted an astonishing 31 goals each as Sunderland won the League title. In between winning these trophies, Carter had scored the winner as Arsenal were beaten in the Charity Shield.

CARTER

Carter was class personified. His passing was razor sharp with Raich possessing the vision to know where and when to deliver the ball. His shooting was accurate and fierce with either foot and his ability to read the game was top drawer. In Sunderland's great team of the thirties, there is no dispute that maestro Carter was the stand-out player in an outstanding side.

FULL NAME:
Horatio Stratton Carter

POSITION:
Inside-forward

DATE OF BIRTH:
21 December 1913

PLACE OF BIRTH:
Sunderland

SUNDERLAND DEBUT:
Sheffield Wednesday 3-1 Sunderland
15 October 1932

APPEARANCES:
278

GOALS:
128

Six of his best seasons were lost to the Second World War. He'd scored three goals in the only three games played of the 1939/40 season. These were expunged from the records when the season was cancelled with the declaration of war.

Two of those goals were in an opening day win over Derby County who he would play for as a 'Guest' during the war and sign for after it. Winning the FA Cup with the Rams in 1946, Carter became the only player to win the cup both before and after World War Two.

Raich went on to play for Hull City - winning Division Three North - and Cork Athletic, with whom he won the FA of Ireland Cup in 1953. At Hull he was player/manager and he continued in management with Leeds United, Mansfield Town and Middlesbrough, guiding the first two of those clubs to promotion.

At international level he scored four times against England at Roker Park for 'The Rest' as he humiliated the national side to the tune of 7-1 in March 1934. The following month he was selected for his international debut in a 3-0 win over Scotland at Wembley. It was the first of 13 full caps Carter won over a period of 13 years and 34 days. Of course, had it not been for the war he would have won many more. The gap of nine years and 164 days between his sixth and seventh caps was the third longest ever.

CARTER

Carter scored seven times for his country and netted another 17 in 18 war-time games for England. He also represented the Football League four times and the League of Ireland twice. In total he scored 387 goals in 696 appearances.

Not content with that, he also played Minor Counties cricket for Durham and three first class county matches for Derbyshire.

FULL NAME:
Brian Howard Clough

POSITION:
Centre forward

DATE OF BIRTH:
21 March 1935

PLACE OF BIRTH:
Middlesbrough

SUNDERLAND DEBUT:
Walsall 4-3 Sunderland
19 August 1961

APPEARANCES:
74

GOALS:
63

One of the most famous managers the game has seen, Brian Clough reached legendary status as a centre-forward with Sunderland, and before that Middlesbrough.

Of forwards to score over 200 goals in their careers, no-one in the history of the game has a better goals to games ratio than Clough. At Sunderland he netted 63 goals in 74 games to add to the 204 in 222 games he bagged for Boro, in all competitions.

On Teesside he'd scored at least 40 goals in four successive seasons from 1956/57 to 1959/60, and had been capped by England against Wales and Sweden in October 1959. In September 1960 he scored the only goal of the game for Boro against Sunderland on Teesside.

A fee of £45,000 brought Brian up the A19 in the summer of 1961. A goalscoring debut set the tone as he went on to score 34 goals in 43 games (including five hat-tricks) in what was his only full season at Sunderland. That tally stood as the club's post war record until Kevin Phillips passed it in 1997/98. With all due respect to SuperKev, he might have had an even tougher challenge had Clough not suffered what proved to be a career ending cruciate ligament injury mid-way through his second season.

Cloughie had scored 28 goals in 28 games when he was injured on Boxing Day. Chasing a long ball on a frosty pitch he collided with Bury 'keeper Chris Harker.

CLOUGH

Shakers centre-half Bob Stokoe infamously accused Clough of kidding, but in fact the game had just lost one of its greatest goalscorers.

A season-and-a-half later Brian attempted a come-back. Over 45,000 had attended the previous home game when Sunderland returned to the top-flight after a six-year absence. Almost 7,000 more attended the second home game v West Brom to see Clough's comeback.

FULL NAME:
Brian Howard Clough

POSITION:
Centre forward

DATE OF BIRTH:
21 March 1935

PLACE OF BIRTH:
Middlesbrough

SUNDERLAND DEBUT:
Walsall 4-3 Sunderland
19 August 1961

APPEARANCES:
74

GOALS:
63

He would manage only three appearances before realising he would have to retire. What proved to be the only top-flight goal of his career came in the second of that trio of games, against Leeds United, a team he would later controversially manage.

In the season he suffered his injury, Clough commenced with a brace in an opening day win over his former club and had scored two hat-tricks and seven braces by the time he was struck down. The last goal before his injury, appropriately enough, had come at Ayresome Park against 'Boro. Sunderland were in a promotion position when their star striker was injured.

Come the end of the season, they missed out on promotion on goal average, finishing level with second placed Chelsea and just a point behind champions Stoke. Surely had Clough not been injured they would have gone up then rather than a year later?

Having moved into coaching at Sunderland, Clough moved into management at Hartlepool in October 1965 - with his Sunderland youth team en route to the first of three FA Youth Cup finals in four years. At Hartlepool. Clough lifted the perennial strugglers to eighth, which led to a move to Derby County.

He took the Rams from the second division to the semi-final of the European Cup - having won the league title to qualify at a time when only the champions qualified for the continent's top tournament.

CLOUGH

Next came brief spells with Brighton and Leeds before he began what would be an 18-year era as manager at Nottingham Forest, beginning in 1975. Clough led Forest to promotion, the league title, four League Cups and two European Cups amidst a host of other honours and finals. He twice had the chance to manage Sunderland under the chairmanship of Keith Collings and Tom Cowie, but sadly at Sunderland the ever-colourful and controversial Clough will always be known as a player - but what a player!

Think of the great side of the 1930s and you probably think of Raich Carter, Bobby Gurney and perhaps Johnny Mapson. There were other great players in the team though, none more than left-winger Jimmy Connor, who despite the hugely successful players around him, was for many the darling of the crowd.

Connor ripped full-backs apart with his pace and as well as making plenty of goals for Sunderland's record goalscorer Gurney, liked to cut in and fire home a shot himself. If one word summed up Connor it would be 'effective'. Jimmy always had a purpose, he liked to see the ball in the back of the net, whether he'd made the goal or scored it. He wasn't one for beating a player too or three times to demonstrate his mastery of either the opponent or the ball, once he'd beaten a man he'd be taking on the next one or delivering a cross or shot.

In the end, rough play did for him. Always the target of heavy tackling, he was eventually put out of the game when barely 30. Injury cost him a cup medal in 1937, but he'd been ever -present when the league was won a year earlier. His seven goals that season made him the only member of the five man forward line not to hit double figures, but he made plenty and scored not only the last goal of the season, but arguably the most important, the winner in a nine-goal thriller with deposed champions Arsenal.

CONNOR

Later a season ticket holder at Sunderland, the Scottish international was one of the men who made Sunderland great.

FULL NAME:
James Connor

POSITION:
Outside-left

DATE OF BIRTH:
1 June 1909

PLACE OF BIRTH:
Renfrew

SUNDERLAND DEBUT:
Sunderland 3–3 Manchester City
30 August 1930

APPEARANCES:
283

GOALS:
61

FULL NAME:
John Andrew Crossan

POSITION:
Inside-forward

DATE OF BIRTH:
29 November 1938

PLACE OF BIRTH:
Londonderry

SUNDERLAND DEBUT:
Sunderland 6-2 Grimsby Town
3 November 1962

APPEARANCES:
99

GOALS:
48

Top scorer in the much loved first ever promotion team of 1964, Johnny Crossan was a Northern Ireland international with a razor sharp knack of cleanly connecting with his expertly directed efforts on goal.

He had experienced European Cup football before coming to Sunderland, playing against Real Madrid in the semi-final just a few months before coming to Roker Park. Signed by Alan Brown from Standard Liege, Crossan had gained earlier continental experience with Sparta Rotterdam. His time in the Low Countries came about as his attempt to move into English football from Ireland - where he had played for Derry City and Coleraine - was thwarted due to accusations of taking payment when a teenage amateur.

Manager Brown was a stickler for discipline, but was no-one's fool and wasted no time in capturing Crossan, once sanctions limiting his opportunities in British football expired.

A hat-trick by Brian Clough on his debut augured well as Crossan slotted into an exciting side, but Clough would suffer his serious injury before Crossan got his name in the paper as a scorer. Johnny didn't score in his first nine games, but netted 15 in his next 20.

In his first full season he was ever-present as promotion was won, being top scorer with 22 in the league plus another five in the cup, including a celebrated brace away to cup holders Manchester United in the quarter-final. In the top flight Clough's aborted comeback saw him play three times, the only top-flight goal of his

CROSSAN

career being accompanied by two from Crossan against old adversaries Leeds.

The appointment of George Hardwick as manager was followed shortly afterwards by Crossan's sale to Manchester City, who he captained to the Division Two title in 1966 before playing for Middlesbrough and returning to Belgian football.

Half of his 24 caps for Northern Ireland were won with Sunderland.

Stan Cummins was a skilful winger who cost Sunderland a club record £300,000 a third of the way through the 1979/80 season and immediately delivered on the investment.

A scoring debut was the first of a dozen goals in 26 league appearances in what proved to be a promotion-winning season, with Cummins scoring on the night promotion was won. In between his first and last Sunderland games of that initial Wearside campaign, he bagged four in one game against Burnley and hit the winner in what proved to be the last home win over Newcastle in a ridiculously long 28-year period without a home win over the Magpies.

At only 5'6" with a light-weight frame, Cummins had a low centre of gravity and subsequently great balance which allowed him to ride many of the rough challenges that came his way in an era when defenders had much more licence to lame than they do now. His trickery on the ball, allied to his determination made Stan a crowd favourite and he played more than twice as many games for Sunderland than his other two English clubs combined.

Sedgefield born, Stan started with Middlesbrough who he joined as an 11-year-old, discovered by the man who also discovered Brian Clough, 'Boro scout Ray Grant. A first-teamer at 17, Cummins made his first venture across the Atlantic to play for Minnesota Kicks while still a teenager.

CUMMINS

Such was Stan's enjoyment of soccer Stateside that by the time he hung up his boots he had played only 18 fewer league games in America than the 222 he totted up on this side of the pond.

In the summer of 1981, Sunderland allowed him to spend the summer turning out 15 times for Seattle Sounders. Can you imagine a top-flight club allowing a player they'd spent a record fee on doing that now?

FULL NAME:
Stanley Cummins

POSITION:
Winger/midfielder

DATE OF BIRTH:
6 December 1958

PLACE OF BIRTH:
Sedgefield

SUNDERLAND DEBUT:
Sunderland 3-1 Notts County
17 November 1979

APPEARANCES:
159 (6)

GOALS:
32

Later after a second spell with Sunderland ended, Cummins played extensively for Minnesota Strikers, followed by Kansas City Comets, finishing in 1989, a decade after arriving at Roker Park.

That second spell at Sunderland seemed a long way off when Cummins controversially brought his first stint to a close. Having helped the side to promotion in 1980 he'd continued to do well, being Player of the Year in his first full season. The only ever-present in the first year back in the top flight, he scored a memorable last-day winner at Anfield to beat Liverpool and help keep Sunderland up. It was his tenth goal of a season in which he'd scored in the first two games as Sunderland topped the embryonic top-flight table. After missing the start of the following season as a result of his Seattle sojourn, Stan still played 35 games in 1981/82 and appeared a further 30 times for Alan Durban's steadily improving side in 1982/83.

It was at this point that Cummins - having been offered a contract that did not improve on his existing one - found himself entitled to a free transfer, an option which he exercised in dropping a division to join Crystal Palace. In the capital though Cummins managed just two league appearances for each of the 14 months he spent at Selhurst Park before re-signing for Sunderland in October 1984. A month earlier he scored for Palace at Sunderland in the Milk Cup but found himself cup-tied when returning and watched from the sidelines as Sunderland reached the Wembley final.

CUMMINS

As he made his second Sunderland 'debut' his new/old club were seventh in the top flight, but neither Stan nor Sunderland could re-kindle the magic. Cummins failed to score in his 17 appearances as Sunderland went down, Stan's last appearance coming in a tepid 0-4 home defeat by Aston Villa. At the age of 26 Stan Cummins had played his last competitive game in English football.

FULL NAME:
Stanley Cummins

POSITION:
Winger/midfielder

DATE OF BIRTH:
6 December 1958

PLACE OF BIRTH:
Sedgefield

SUNDERLAND DEBUT:
Sunderland 3-1 Notts County
17 November 1979

APPEARANCES:
159 (6)

GOALS:
32

Top scorer in the top flight in 1950, Dickie Davis did as much as anyone to bring Sunderland as close as they have come to a post-war top division title.

Davis hit 25 goals in 34 games (plus three in two cup appearances) as Sunderland finished a point behind the champions. Had their spearhead not missed five of the last six games, his goal-touch might well have brought a seventh league title to Wearside. If so, then the Bank of England team of the decade to come, might have produced the sort of dividends they spectacularly failed to deliver given the club's outlay on talent.

Three of those late-season games Davis missed were lost, including a monumentally disastrous home defeat to eventually relegated Manchester City. When Davis did return on the last day of the season, he scored twice in a big win over Chelsea, but it was too late.

Born in the Aston area of Birmingham, Dickie played as a war-time 'Guest' player for Aston Villa during World War Two. He had joined Sunderland a month after his 17th birthday in 1939 only for the outbreak of war to result in him having to wait until seven years after signing before he could make his full debut, duly marking his home debut with a goal against Liverpool a week later. Gradually establishing himself, Dickie's best season wasn't enough to provide him with a long-term first team place. A slow start the following campaign, when he scored just twice in his

DAVIS

first eight games, saw him shoved aside from centre-forward to inside forward as Sunderland splashed the cash for the record signing of Trevor Ford.

Ford was a fabulous forward and deserving of his status as a Sunderland hero, but the fact is he never scored as many goals in a season for the Lads as Davis, a terrific goalscorer who moved on to Darlington in 1954 at the age of 32.

FULL NAME:
Richard Daniel Davis

POSITION:
Centre-forward/Inside-right

DATE OF BIRTH:
22 January 1922

PLACE OF BIRTH:
Birmingham

SUNDERLAND DEBUT:
Leeds United 1-1 Sunderland
7 December 1946

APPEARANCES:
154

GOALS:
80

A pedigree striker on the cusp of moving into the top ten of Premier League top scorers as the 2016/17 season kicked off, Defoe came to Sunderland in January 2015.

A top player for over a decade, when based in the south of England, Defoe had departed the Premier League to play in Toronto. Some feared he might be a mere shadow of the player he once was, as he returned to English football in exchange for USA international centre-forward Jozy Altidore, who had found Premier League goals hard to come by.

Swapping Jozy for Jermain was one of the finest bits of business Sunderland have conducted in recent years. Defoe became an instant hero when scoring one of the best goals ever seen in a derby match to beat Newcastle soon after he arrived, before being named Player of the Year in his first full season as his goals kept Sunderland up.

Goals have always been Defoe's stock in trade, but it wasn't just his finishing ability that endeared Jermain to the red and white army. In his first campaign under Dick Advocaat he demonstrated an unheralded aspect of his game, tirelessly working back from the unfamiliar wide position he was asked to operate in. At Arsenal on the night Advocaat shed tears as Sunderland earned the point that kept them up, Defoe had worked as hard as anyone as a goalless draw was battled for.

DEFOE

Jermain had had tears of his own as the enormity of scoring in a Wear-Tyne derby sunk in. His joy in running half the length of the pitch before collapsing; seemingly under the weight of his own tears, became the iconic image of the season. Moments earlier a sumptuously spectacular volley had sealed his place in Wearside folklore.

FULL NAME:
Jermain Colin Defoe

POSITION:
Striker

DATE OF BIRTH:
7 October 1982

PLACE OF BIRTH:
Beckton, London

SUNDERLAND DEBUT:
Tottenham Hotspur 2-1 Sunderland
17 January 2015

APPEARANCES:
48 (5)*

GOALS:
22*

*CORRECT AS OF 30.06.16

Defoe would score against the Magpies again. Had he not done so and had Newcastle won that game instead of drawing it, come the end of the season it would have been the Wearsiders rather than the Tynesiders who slipped to relegation, had all the remaining results panned out as they did.

That strike at St. James' was one of 18 Defoe detonated during a most productive season. 15 of those goals came in the Premier League. Only Kevin Phillips and Darren Bent had surpassed that tally for the Black Cats at top level since the re-structuring of the leagues, while it was a Premier League tally, Defoe had bettered only once.

Despite only Harry Kane and Jamie Vardy, who played in teams who finished third and first, being the only English players to score more than Defoe - whose ammunition was supplied by a team who only just escaped demotion - he was overlooked for an England recall for the 2016 European Championships.

Earlier in his career Jermain had managed 19 international goals in 55 games, a figure all the more impressive as in only three of those games did he play the full 90 minutes. No one has scored as many goals off the bench for England as Defoe who netted seven times from 34 games as a substitute to add to his 12 in 19 starts, giving him a goal for every 123 minutes

DEFOE

played at international level, highly creditable in the modern era.

To the end of June 2016, Jermain's 2010 hat-trick against Bulgaria remained the most recent scored by an England player.

FULL NAME:
Jermain Colin Defoe

POSITION:
Striker

DATE OF BIRTH:
7 October 1982

PLACE OF BIRTH:
Beckton, London

SUNDERLAND DEBUT:
Tottenham Hotspur 2-1 Sunderland
17 January 2015

APPEARANCES:
48 (5)*

GOALS:
22*

*CORRECT AS OF 30.06.16

55

Sunderland's record appearance maker for six decades until overtaken by Len Ashurst, Doig remains third on the all time list. In Doig's day, lucrative friendlies were played throughout the season, so in fact Doig made many more than his 457 competitive appearances.

The club won their first-ever league points on his debut as he kept a first-ever clean sheet - only for the points to be docked and the club fined as the Scotland international had not been properly registered. Known as Ned elsewhere, but more commonly as Ted or Teddy on Wearside, Doig went on to become one of only two men (with Jimmy Millar) to win four league championship medals with Sunderland.

The first three of those were won under manager Tom Watson who he later followed to Liverpool where he was part of the Merseyside club's first-ever top-flight winning team. Doig and Watson are buried near each other in Anfield cemetery.

Doig would famously chase his cap rather than the ball if his headgear blew off as he was so self-conscious about his baldness. On another occasion he threatened a teammate with a table knife on a train returning from an away game, when the half bottle of wine he was entitled to with his meal was stolen. Doig was in the habit of taking it home to have with his Sunday dinner.

DOIG

Not a man to be messed with, Doig was a strong, determined and confident goalkeeper who gave Sunderland great service in the age of 'The Team of All The Talents.' - the greatest team the club have ever had.

FULL NAME:
John Edward Doig

POSITION:
Goalkeeper

DATE OF BIRTH:
29 October 1866

PLACE OF BIRTH:
Letham, Forfarshire

SUNDERLAND DEBUT:
West Bromwich Albion 0-4 Sunderland
20 September 1890

APPEARANCES:
457

FULL NAME:
Trevor Ford

POSITION:
Centre-forward

DATE OF BIRTH:
1 October 1923

PLACE OF BIRTH:
Swansea

SUNDERLAND DEBUT:
Chelsea 3-0 Sunderland
28 October 1950

APPEARANCES:
117

GOALS:
70

Look at that goals to games record: 70 in 117 games. Great value after a world record transfer fee of £29,500 brought the Wales international from Aston Villa, where he'd banged in 61 goals in 128 games.

As a teenager, Ford worked in a blast furnace in his native Swansea where he commenced his professional career and he remained hot in front of goal throughout his playing days. He could be strong-willed too. His failure to get on with teammate Len Shackleton is well documented, while he sued the Wales FA when they left him out of their 1958 World Cup squad after he'd admitted taking illegal payments from Sunderland in the era of the maximum wage. While at Sunderland, he sold cars in the afternoon for the chairman - a good job for a man named Ford.

Trevor also sued the ex-England goalkeeper Gil Merrick when Merrick criticised Ford for being rough on goalkeepers in his autobiography. Ford pointed out that he'd never even been booked let alone sent off, won his case, was awarded damages and had the book withdrawn. Mind you, this was at a time when players could charge 'keepers and indeed on Ford's home debut for Sunderland one of his goals in a hat-trick saw him barge Sheffield Wednesday custodian Dave McIntosh over the goal -line. It wasn't just the goalkeeper, but the goal itself who could suffer from Ford's ferociousness, in that home debut he also managed to dislodge one of the goalposts!

FORD

Brave to the last, on one occasion, in those days of no substitutes, Ford hobbled on the wing playing with a broken ankle in a cup replay at Scunthorpe ...and still scored the winner.

For his country, Ford netted 23 goals in 38 games, two of those goals coming against England at Roker Park in 1950. He also played for Swansea, Cardiff and Newport County as well as having a spell with PSV Eindhoven, after he was banned by the FA following the illegal payments scandal at Roker.

When your first name is enough to make you an instantly recognisable hero you know you've done well - especially if the superfluous surname is as exotic as Gabbiadini.

Although the moniker suggests Marco was an overseas import, he was Nottingham born and a product of York City's youth system, albeit with an Italian father and a brother who played once for Sunderland - Ricardo coming on as sub for Marco, thereby the pair never playing together at first-team level for the Wearsiders.

In a career that brought 222 league goals in 654 Football League games for ten different clubs, it is astonishing that Marco's solitary medal in the game was the third division title won in his first season at Sunderland. Having earned the nickname Marco-Goalo, opposition 'keepers were no strangers to picking the ball out of their net when Marco was about. With a nickname reminiscent of one of the world's great explorers, Marco did his bit of travelling too with a brief stint in Greece that yielded four goals in 11 games for Panionios a decade after arriving at Sunderland.

It was while Gabbiadini was with Sunderland that he earned international recognition, picking up two Under-21 caps and representing England at 'B' level against Czechoslovakia at Roker Park in 1990, in a season when he powered Sunderland into the top flight. It was a second promotion in three years, claimed despite a Play-Off final loss to Swindon Town who were subsequently penalised for financial irregularities.

GABBIADINI

In the semi-finals Sunderland had overcome local rivals Newcastle. Marco had won a last minute penalty in the goalless first leg only for Paul Hardyman to have his shot saved. The second leg however highlighted the power of what was known as the 'G-Force.'

Partnerships are vital in football and Gabbiadini's link up with veteran England forward Eric Gates was sublime.

FULL NAME:
Marco Gabbiadini

POSITION:
Striker

DATE OF BIRTH:
20 January 1968

PLACE OF BIRTH:
Nottingham

SUNDERLAND DEBUT:
Sunderland 0-2 Chester City
26 August 1987

APPEARANCES:
183 (2)

GOALS:
87

FULL NAME:
Marco Gabbiadini

POSITION:
Striker

DATE OF BIRTH:
20 January 1968

PLACE OF BIRTH:
Nottingham

SUNDERLAND DEBUT:
Sunderland 0-2 Chester City
26 August 1987

APPEARANCES:
183 (2)

GOALS:
87

Schemer Gates had the ability to supply speed-merchant Marco with the ammunition and 'Gabbers' needed no second invitation to leave defenders trailing in his wake.

Having given Sunderland the lead in that Play-Off on Tyneside, Gates played in Gabbiadini to wrap up victory in one of the most important derby games ever for Marco's most iconic goal from his time at Sunderland, for whom he scored more goals than any of his other clubs. Top scorer in all four of his full SAFC seasons, Marco became the only player to be Player of the Year in consecutive years, taking the award in 1988/89 and 1989/90, playing a total of 59 competitive games in the second of those campaigns.

Tragically transferred - in the eyes of the fans who idolised him - to Crystal Palace in September 1991, Marco-Goalo had hit a hat-trick away to Charlton on his penultimate Sunderland appearance.

The first hat-trick of Marco's career came when he was just 18 and with his first club York City. It was his former York manager Denis Smith who signed him for Sunderland, the first of many moves. Following his time at Roker Park Gabbiadin's stint at Crystal Palace was short-lived, but was followed by a successful five-year spell at Derby for whom he played more games than anyone else. Brief loans to Birmingham City and Oxford United preceded his Greek adventure with Panionos before a return to home shores with Stoke City, swiftly followed by a loan back to his first club York. Having reached 30 and with experience and strength now going

GABBIADINI

some way to compensate for the relative lack of pace compared to his youth, Marco demonstrated his continued love of the game with successful periods at Darlington and Northampton Town. before ending his playing days with Hartlepool United.

A successful hotelier in York, Marco has always been articulate and opinionated and in recent years has always been a voice worth listening to on BBC Newcastle's Total Sport.

Patsy Gallacher was a key member of a fantastic forward line, one that inspired Sunderland to win the top flight, the Charity Shield and the FA Cup in the space of 12 months.

It was certainly the forward line rather than the defence that won the league for Sunderland. The title was won despite conceding 74 goals in 42 games - more than any team in the top half. A classic example was when the champions of the previous three seasons Arsenal came to Roker and Gallacher was one of the scorers as Sunderland scored five, but only edged victory as four were leaked at the other end.

Born in Bridge of Weir, as an inside-forward Gallacher was indeed a bridge between the two halves in a team based on the old W M formation. Gallacher contributed guile and graft. He worked hard for the team and had the talent to live in the company of his fellow inside-forward, the incomparable Raich Carter. He also linked majestically with his fellow Scots winger Jimmy Connor as well as Alex Hastings, and sometimes Sandy McNab, at left-half.

Gallacher came to Sunderland in 1927, initially as an amateur. Breaking into the team when he had just turned 20, Patsy gradually established himself in the side to the point where he became indispensable. Primarily a goal-maker, his record of better than a goal per three games included half-a-dozen hat-tricks.

GALLACHER

In the title winning 1935/36 campaign Patsy notched 19 in 37 games plus another from two cup appearances. A year later when the cup was won Patsy played in all nine games scoring three times including the winner in the semi-final.

Despite scoring on his Scotland debut in 1934, he won just the one cap. He deserved more but had a full set of medals from English football in his time at Sunderland.

FULL NAME:
Patrick Gallacher

POSITION:
Inside-forward

DATE OF BIRTH:
21 August 1909

PLACE OF BIRTH:
Bridge of Weir, Renfrewshire

SUNDERLAND DEBUT:
Sunderland 0-1 Arsenal
21 September 1929

APPEARANCES:
308

GOALS:
107

FULL NAME:
Robert Gurney

POSITION:
Centre-forward

DATE OF BIRTH:
13 October 1907

PLACE OF BIRTH:
Silksworth

SUNDERLAND DEBUT:
West Ham United 3-2 Sunderland
3 April 1926

APPEARANCES:
390

GOALS:
228

Over 1,000 players have turned out for Sunderland. None of them have scored as many goals for the club as Bobby Gurney.

Indeed, fewer than ten per cent can say they played as many games for the club as the number of goals scored by Gurney. Bobby was renowned for never giving up, Gurney was the grafter's grafter. He was also a goal machine. He scored nine on his reserve team debut and marked his first-team debut at the age of 18 by getting on the score-sheet.

Bobby's first home game saw him in the forward-line alongside the man with the best-ever goals to game ratio in Sunderland colours, Davie Halliday. Playing for visitors Arsenal, was Sunderland's all time record scorer, Charlie Buchan, making his first return to Roker Park. Sunderland won 2-1, 'Boy' Gurney getting both of Sunderland's goals.

Buchan would remain Sunderland's record league goal-scorer, but including cup goals, Gurney's eventual tally of 228 would be six more than even Buchan managed. Gurney would develop during the late twenties, despite missing almost exactly a year. A large part of that absence was due to breaking his leg playing for the reserves at Workington in the week he turned 20. As in his home debut, when Bobby returned, Arsenal were the visitors. If there were any doubts that Gurney's goal touch might have deserted him they quickly disappeared - he hit a hat trick!

GURNEY

However, as so often happens after a lengthy injury, Bobby then found the going tough. He didn't get a game at all the following season as Halliday set Sunderland's seasonal scoring record. Bobby's time had to come though and when Halliday was sold Gurney came into his own. Four goals in a 6-0 win over Liverpool at Anfield was the highlight of a season where with 17 goals in 25 games. He became Sunderland's top scorer for the first time.

It would be the first of seven successive seasons where Bobby top-scored, the last of those seeing him joint top-scorer alongside his great friend Raich Carter.

On that occasion Gurney and Carter netted an astonishing 31 goals each as Sunderland stormed to the league championship. On the day the title was sealed, Bobby bagged four at Birmingham in a 7-2 victory. It was the third time in the season Sunderland had scored seven, Gurney having scored five on the previous occasion. Only three other players have gone nap for the Lads, Buchan being the only other to do so in the top flight - 23 years earlier to the day, and on the previous occasion Sunderland became champions.

Champions is what Sunderland became for the sixth time when Gurney received his medal, but while no club at that point had been champions more than the Wearsiders, Sunderland had never won the cup. That would be rectified a year later, Bobby scoring Sunderland's first-ever cup final goal, having scored in the previous three rounds.

The cup would bring Gurney's final appearance for Sunderland two seasons later, Bobby breaking his leg again at Blackburn. World War Two intervened before he was fit again and when football resumed after the war, Bobby joined the coaching staff before moving into management.

Capped once officially by England, Bobby also played and scored for England against Scotland in a King George's Jubilee game for which players received a Loving Cup rather than a cap.

GURNEY

Bobby Gurney will forever be Sunderland's top scorer (Even SuperKev fell almost a century short of Bobby's total) but even more than the magnificent goals record, Bobby Gurney's commitment, modesty and sheer love of the club is the embodiment of what Sunderland is all about.

FULL NAME:
Robert Gurney

POSITION:
Centre-forward

DATE OF BIRTH:
13 October 1907

PLACE OF BIRTH:
Silksworth

SUNDERLAND DEBUT:
West Ham United 3-2 Sunderland
3 April 1926

APPEARANCES:
390

GOALS:
228

FULL NAME:
David Halliday

POSITION:
Centre-forward

DATE OF BIRTH:
19 December 1901

PLACE OF BIRTH:
Dumfries

SUNDERLAND DEBUT:
Sunderland 3-1 Birmingham
29 August 1925

APPEARANCES:
175

GOALS:
165

You need to know just one thing about Dave Halliday - in the worst of his full seasons for Sunderland, he still scored more goals than anyone else has ever done in their best!

He scored twice in each of his first two games in August 1925, but he was just warming up – he scored hat-tricks in each of the next two! Halliday ended that first season with 42 goals in 46 league and cup games, firing Sunderland to third place.

Dave netting 37 times in 34 games in 1926/27. A highlight was a four-goal haul in a 6-0 thrashing of Manchester United that took Sunderland to the top of the table, but despite his best efforts - including two other hat-tricks - the Lads had to settle for third place again.

Halliday scored at least once in each of the opening eight games of his third season. Another hat-trick against Manchester United and another four goal performance (v Portsmouth) brought big wins, but although Halliday bagged 39 goals in 41 games, the defence let in more than the 74 goals the team scored and Sunderland finished in the bottom half.

The Lads would be back up to fourth in 1928/29 when Halliday set the club record for most goals in a season, netting 43 from the 42 games he played in as an ever-present. He evidently liked Manchester United as he scored yet another hat-trick against them, and scored a further two hat-tricks in addition to producing another four-goal display.

He started 1929/30 with a hat-trick in the second game, but there was just one other goal in ten further games before a fee of £6,500 took Halliday to Arsenal. Dave had begun with Queen of the South Wanderers followed by St. Mirren and Dundee before coming south to Sunderland.

HALLIDAY

Later, after leaving Arsenal, he turned out for Manchester City, Folkestone, Clapton Orient and Yeovil & Petters United, where he became player-manager. Before World War Two, he became manager of Aberdeen, leading them to the Scottish Cup in 1947 (He'd played in the 1924 final for Dundee) and the league title in 1955 which led to a move to Leicester City.

As a player, Halliday scored 347 league goals in 464 games and at Leicester managed Arthur Rowley, who with 434 league goals, scored more than anyone in English history.

Rowley surpassed Halliday's SAFC record of 43 with 44 as Halliday managed Leicester to the second division title in 1957. A year later, the Foxes needed to win their last game to stay up and did - thereby condemning Sunderland to their first-ever relegation. Halliday left Leicester, and football, the following October. He passed away in 1970.

FULL NAME:
Martin Harvey

POSITION:
Full-back or midfield

DATE OF BIRTH:
19 September 1941

PLACE OF BIRTH:
Belfast

SUNDERLAND DEBUT:
Plymouth Argyle 0-0 Sunderland
24 October 1959

APPEARANCES:
353 (3)

GOALS:
5

When Martin Harvey stepped out for his League debut at Home Park Plymouth in October 1959, little did the Northern Irishman realise that it would indeed become his home. Harvey settled there in later life after coaching at Argyle.

Harvey holds the record for the most caps won while with Sunderland for any of the home nations. His 34 caps for Northern Ireland began when he was still in his teens. A little over a decade after his final cap Martin was his country's assistant-manager at the 1982 World Cup under Billy Bingham - the man whose record he'd taken - Bingham won 33 Irish caps while with Sunderland. Harvey later worked as assistant to Bingham in Saudi Arabia, having coached at Millwall, Raith Rovers and Carlisle, where he also managed.

Injury put paid to Martin's playing days in 1972 when he was just 30. Just over a year later Sunderland won the FA Cup. He could so easily have been part of the cup winning team. He had played in all 32 league games of the season until his injury and had always been a class act.

A quality player either at left-back or in his preferred wing-half berth, Harvey's talent was such that he displaced legends for both club and country: Stan Anderson for Sunderland and Danny Blanchflower for Northern Ireland. Probably only George Best surpasses Blanchflower in Northern Ireland's football

HARVEY

history, while Len Ashurst is the only outfield player to play more times than Anderson for Sunderland.

A great reader of the game, Harvey hovered over the grass, or so it appeared, such was the smoothness of his movement. If you were a teammate, Martin was the person you wanted to pass to you, such was the weight of his delivery.

Harvey had a Testimonial at Sunderland, against Newcastle in 1975.

FULL NAME:
Alexander Cockburn Hastings

POSITION:
Left-half

DATE OF BIRTH:
17 March 1912

PLACE OF BIRTH:
Falkirk

SUNDERLAND DEBUT:
Portsmouth 1-1 Sunderland
6 September 1930

APPEARANCES:
297

GOALS:
6

The captain of the last Sunderland side to win the top division, Alex Hastings was a high-calibre half-back who provided much of the ammunition to Sunderland's much vaunted forward line of the mid-thirties.

Injuries and a more than able deputy in Sandy McNab, restricted Hastings to 31 of the 42 league games in the championship winning 1935/36 campaign, but while his season was over two games before the title was mathematically sealed, it was Hastings who received the trophy at Roker Park before the final home game of the season. He was just a month past his 24th birthday.

Having arrived from Stenhousemuir, Hastings had been a versatile player as a youth. In schools football, he had started as a full-back, played as a centre-half and then scored over 50 goals in under a season as a centre-forward. Signed by Johnny Cochrane, Hastings' debut came as an 18-year-old, just two games after left-winger Jimmy Connor came into the side. Both would go on to play for Sunderland and as left-half and left-winger they would provide a key partnership in Sunderland's successful side of the thirties, both immediately becoming regulars.

Hastings' only goal in his first seven years was in the club's record (2-7) FA Cup defeat at Aston Villa. After 203 games without a league goal he was picked to lead the attack at Derby and scored. Thereafter he occasionally played up front and ended his career with half-a-dozen goals.

ALEX HASTINGS

World War Two took away six years of his career and denied him the two goals he scored in the three games of the 1939/40 season, which was abandoned with appearances and goals from those games expunged from the records. He then scored in Sunderland's first two post-war games, but only played twice more before retiring. Later emigrating to Australia, he became President of the South Australia Soccer Federation.

Young Player of the Year at Sunderland in 2009/10 and 2010/11, Jordan Henderson's time as a first-teamer at Sunderland was too short. Sold for a reported £16m when he had barely reached the age of 21, this home-grown player won his first England cap against France at Wembley when he was still with Sunderland. By the time he was 26 he had gained as many England caps as his age.

By then Henderson had replaced Anfield legend Steven Gerrard as Liverpool captain, but despite all he had achieved he still divided opinion among many punters and pundits. The men who matter though are those who pick the team and from Roy Keane (who knew a thing or two about playing in midfield and who gave Jordan his debut) to Jurgen Klopp at Liverpool Henderson has been a regular choice whenever available.

In a book like this on Masterpieces it is easy to get carried away with the player who produces a moment of magic every now and then, the sort of player who can provide you with a memory that lasts a lifetime with a classic piece of skill. While you don't get to captain Liverpool and be an England regular without being able to play, Jordan Henderson's value to a team isn't measured in magical moments. Always remembering football is a team game, Hendo is a team player par excellence. Invariably putting side before self, Jordan's unselfishness is easy to overlook, but make no mistake about it, he is top quality,

HENDERSO

even if sometimes the quality of his football is overshadowed by the sheer quantity of his contribution.

One thing is for certain and that is by the time he hangs up his boots, Henderson will have many more than the already impressive 26 caps he has as this book goes to print.

FULL NAME:
Jordan Brian Henderson

POSITION:
Midfield

DATE OF BIRTH:
17 June 1990

PLACE OF BIRTH:
East Herrington

SUNDERLAND DEBUT:
Chelsea 5-0 Sunderland
1 November 2008

APPEARANCES:
67 (12)

GOALS:
5

George Herd had won the Scottish Cup with Clyde in 1958 before moving to Sunderland in 1961 for a sizeable £42,500 fee, debuting on the final day of the 1960/61 season, a week before his 25th birthday.

A Scotland international capped five times with Clyde and previously once at amateur level when with Queen's Park, Herd would gain no further international recognition having crossed the border, but nonetheless he was international class throughout his decade at Roker.

As a player George mixed skill with stamina. Attempts to man-mark him out of games were doomed to failure as he deliberately ran his marker into the ground - and remember for the first few years of his Sunderland career, substitutes weren't allowed.

A maker more than a taker of goals, George was nonetheless second top-scorer in his first full season in England when he created plenty for the team's top scorer - Brian Clough. Two of Herd's haul came in a 3-0 home win over Newcastle. Two seasons later he also contributed the winner at home to Newcastle as one of 16 goals in all competitions as promotion was won. Herd's taste for derby goals continued two years later with one in another home win after Newcastle had joined Sunderland in the top flight.

Playing his final match for Sunderland at Chelsea in 1969, George moved onto the coaching staff, but added 16 more senior games as player-coach at Hartlepool who he joined in June 1970.

HERD

He later coached Newcastle's juniors, managed Queen of the South and coached in Kuwait as well as with Darlington, Middlesbrough and back at Sunderland where he ran the youth team along with his former teammate Jim Montgomery. Such was Herd's dedication to the game he was still coaching Sunderland Ryhope C.A. in the Northern League until his late 70s!

FULL NAME:
George Herd

POSITION:
Inside-right/outside-right

DATE OF BIRTH:
6 May 1936

PLACE OF BIRTH:
Gartcosh, Glasgow

SUNDERLAND DEBUT:
Sunderland 1–1 Liverpool
29 April 1961

APPEARANCES:
315 (3)

GOALS:
55

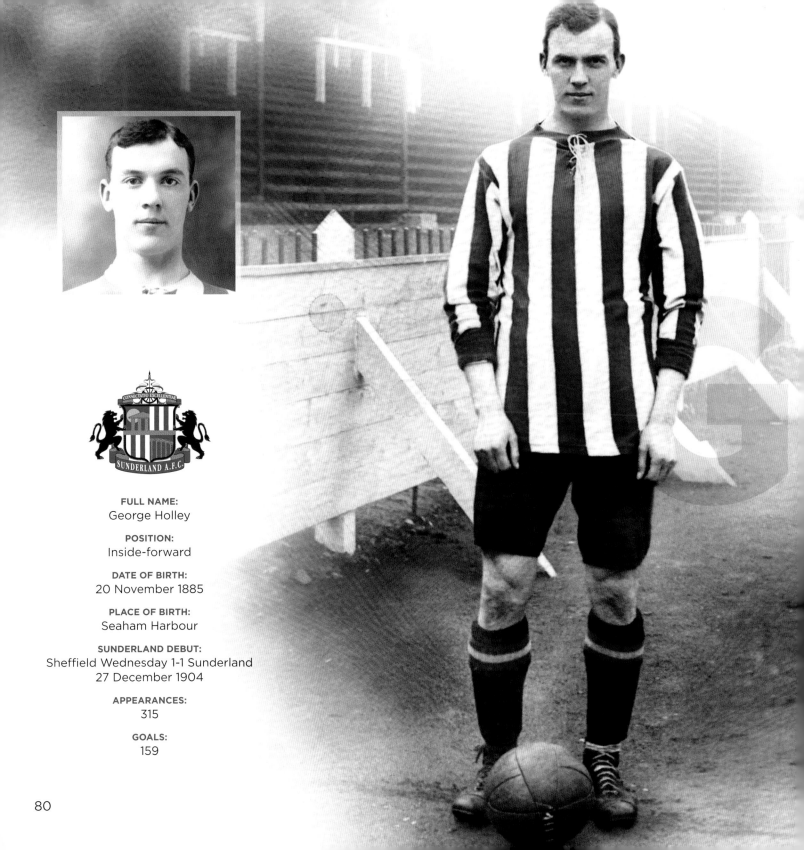

FULL NAME:
George Holley

POSITION:
Inside-forward

DATE OF BIRTH:
20 November 1885

PLACE OF BIRTH:
Seaham Harbour

SUNDERLAND DEBUT:
Sheffield Wednesday 1-1 Sunderland
27 December 1904

APPEARANCES:
315

GOALS:
159

No player has scored more goals for England while on Sunderland's books than Holley. Seven decades before Seaham's famous son Gary Rowell scored a hat-trick at Newcastle, this fellow Seaham lad also scored three at Newcastle - in the record 9-1 away win.

Holley also won the league title and played in the FA Cup final for Sunderland. They may well have won that 1913 cup final if not for Holley - not that it was George's fault! Holley was injured and in a team picture taken on the morning of the final he can be seen wearing football boots instead of shoes as he and his teammates are pictured in smart suits.

Holley had been having a fitness test. It had been decided he wouldn't be fit to play, but when his replacement, Walter Tinsley saw the size of the crowd (over 120,000, a gate only topped once in the history of English football), nerves got the better of him and he couldn't play, leaving Holley to hobble through 90 minutes in the days long before substitutes were allowed.

Holley had scored the winner in the semi-final, one of 17 goals he scored that season out of a total of 159 he registered for the club. Only Bobby Gurney, Charlie Buchan and Davie Halliday have scored more. Holley was top-scorer or joint top-scorer on six occasions.

HOLLEY

A brilliant ball player with sublime control, Holley is one of ten players featured on the wall of the biggest meeting room in Black Cat House.

In ten England appearances he scored eight times, including braces in big wins away to Hungary and Austria and one against Scotland in Glasgow when he was up against clubmate Charlie Thomson. After World War One he coached Sunderland while his son Tom played for Barnsley and Leeds.

81

FULL NAME:
Charles Joseph Hurley

POSITION:
Centre-half

DATE OF BIRTH:
4 October 1936

PLACE OF BIRTH:
Cork

SUNDERLAND DEBUT:
Blackpool 7-0 Sunderland
5 October 1957

APPEARANCES:
400 (1)

GOALS:
26

Voted Sunderland's Player of the Century and renowned in song as 'The Greatest Centre-Half the World has ever seen' Charlie Hurley to many is still known simply as the King.

Accompanying Sunderland as guest ambassador on a pre-season tour of Ireland in 2007 while his fellow Corkman Roy Keane was Sunderland manager, the pair got into a taxi. Keane of course is revered in Cork and was described as the king, "There's only one king in Cork' boomed Charlie - in his southern English accent, Hurley having left the city of his birthplace at the age of seven months as his parents moved to Rainham in Essex where he was brought up.

Regardless of where he was raised, Charlie is fiercely proud of being from Ireland for whom he played 40 times, and equally proud of his loyalty for Sunderland, for whom he played ten times as much. While his fans loved the King, Charlie's loyalty to his 'subjects' has always been just as passionate. Hurley takes every opportunity to express his love of the fans and undoubtedly his place in red and white folklore is assured.

Until Seb Larsson surpassed his achievement in recent years, Charlie was Sunderland's most capped international player, winning all but the first and last of his 40 caps while based on Wearside.

HURLEY

Having had a trial with Arsenal as a 15-year-old and had the chance to sign for West Ham, Charlie began his senior career with Millwall, debuting in a Third Division South fixture at Torquay in January 1954. It was at the same ground just over two-and-a-half years later that Charlie scored his first goal, albeit in a 7-2 defeat.

Seven goals would also be conceded by Sunderland on Hurley's debut at Blackpool just over a year later. It wasn't much of a birthday present for Charlie who had turned 21 the day before.

Charlie famously noted Sunderland were improving after his second appearance when a 6-0 reverse was suffered at Burnley. Fans in the 34,676 crowd who saw Charlie's home debut against Preston must have wondered about the new-boy signed by manager Alan Brown, a former centre-half himself. Hurley however, had done well on a personal level after a Jan Kirchhoff style nightmare on his first appearance and in front of his home crowd, played his part in ensuring a clean-sheet.

Yet to be anointed, Charlie soon built a solid reputation at Roker, although he was unable to prevent the club suffering a first-ever relegation. Part of Hurley's legend was his ability in the opposition's penalty area rather than his own, but it was over three years after his debut before he found the back of the net.

It was Boxing Day 1960 at home to Sheffield United that Charlie changed the face of football. Trailing 1-0 to the Blades, captain Stan Anderson told Charlie to move forward for a corner. Until then centre-halves didn't go up for corners, but Charlie scored, did so again in the next home game and soon the sight of Hurley moving forward was a highlight of the match. In an era when crowds didn't chant as they do now, Roker would roar 'Charlie, Charlie' as the big man strode forward.

HURLEY

A towering presence who played the beautiful game, preferring to pass than pelt it forward, Charlie took over as captain when Anderson left, leading the club to promotion in 1964 when he was runner-up to Bobby Moore as Footballer of the Year.

The King had another five years at the club, finally bowing out in 1969, moving to Bolton where a young Sam Allardyce was in the youth team.

FULL NAME:
Charles Joseph Hurley

POSITION:
Centre-half

DATE OF BIRTH:
4 October 1936

PLACE OF BIRTH:
Cork

SUNDERLAND DEBUT:
Blackpool 7-0 Sunderland
5 October 1957

APPEARANCES:
400 (1)

GOALS:
26

'Magic' Johnston's trademark was the curler into the top corner from around the angle of the box. A 'jinky' winger who could drop the shoulder and make the man trying to mark him slip a disc, Allan Johnston could tie defenders up in knots.

He had no great pace, but didn't need it. Behind him left-back Mickey Gray dovetailed with him perfectly and time after time would steam past Allan, who would roll an exquisitely weighted ball into his path.

Called up by Scotland at the peak of his performance levels at Sunderland, he was a treat to watch and one of the reasons those early seasons at the Stadium of Light were so joyous.

Johnston had joined shortly before the closure of Roker Park and wrote his name into the record books by scoring the last competitive goal at the ground against Everton. Two years later he signed-off with a goal not in the record books.

This time it was against the other half of Merseyside in a game to commemorate one hundred seasons of the Football League, Sunderland being invited to participate as they had just won the trophy. Johnno though, would not play again after a contract dispute, which was such a pity as seeing him as part of the '105 point team' in the top flight was eagerly awaited.

JOHNSTON

Allan no doubt had to deal with such contract problems himself after moving into management with Queen of the South, Kilmarnock and Dunfermline.

FULL NAME:
Allan Johnston

POSITION:
Winger

DATE OF BIRTH:
14 December 1973

PLACE OF BIRTH:
Glasgow

SUNDERLAND DEBUT:
Newcastle United 1-1 Sunderland
5 April 1997

APPEARANCES:
96 (5)

GOALS:
20

Signed from French football where he had spent the previous couple of years playing for Bordeaux following five years with Bastia, Wahbi Khazri is a bag of tricks as a footballer, the sort of player who is always prepared to try something different and lift people off their seats.

He was one of the players brought in by Sam Allardyce in January of 2016 as Sunderland needed a lift to help them climb away from trouble. Khazri - along with fellow new boys Lamine Kone and Jan Kirchhoff - made light of the common belief that players from abroad need a settling-in period when they arrive in English football.

Khazri was part of a trio who provided Sunderland with a serious injection of quality. What was noticeable about Wahbi (as well as the others) was his willingness to get stuck in. Clearly a player with ample ability, he endeared himself to the crowd by the way he worked hard for the team in addition to the way in which he tried to use the ball when he got it.

An early game against Manchester United brought reward when Khazri's floated free-kick deceived goalkeeper David de Gea and crept in and De Gea was undone again later when he was unable to keep out Kone's header for what proved to be a dramatic winner from Khazri's corner.

KHAZRI

If the crowd lapped that up it was nothing compared to a thrilling late season five goal thriller with Chelsea which Sunderland edged, aided in no small measure by a 'goal of the season' quality volley from Wahbi who will do well to ever score a better goal.

Moving into his first full season the Tunisian international hoped to produce many more masterpiece moments in red and white.

FULL NAME:
Wahbi Khazri

POSITION:
Midfield/forward

DATE OF BIRTH:
8 February 1991

PLACE OF BIRTH:
Ajaccio, Corsica, France

SUNDERLAND DEBUT:
Sunderland 0-1 Manchester City
2 February 2016

APPEARANCES:
14*

GOALS:
2*

*CORRECT AS OF 30.06.16

89

There are many players who have enjoyed great debuts. Jan Kirchhoff isn't one of them, but neither was Charlie Hurley, the 'Player of the Century' who was hammered 7-0 on his first appearance!

Things weren't quite so disastrous for Kirchhoff, but they were bad enough, as after coming off the bench with Sunderland level at White Hart Lane, the tall German conceded a penalty and saw another goal go in off him in what finished as a dismal 4-1 reverse.

Supporters expectations of Kirchhoff were low after that, but he rapidly changed opinions with a series of highly accomplished displays, none more so than in a derby at Newcastle when his imperious display could have drawn not unreasonable comparisons with probably the greatest German player of them all, Franz Beckenbauer. Soon Kirchhoff was winning the PFA Fans Player of the Month award for April as his displays helped Sunderland to successfully stave off the threat of relegation. Operating in front of the back four, Jan's coolness in possession, allied to his effortless passing and a sheer talent for nicking the ball away from opponents, meant he quickly became a major influence for the Black Cats' re-shaped side.

Coming to England represented a fresh start for a player who having been capped by Germany up to U21 level, had found his career hindered by injury. Having made his senior debut for Mainz 05 in 2008 by the time of his 2013 move to Bayern Munich the German powerhouse's move for him was based more on quality

KIRCHHOFF

than quantity, Kirchhoff having made only 58 appearances for Mainz. Before the end of 2013 Bayern had loaned him to Schalke for 18 months. During that time he made six Champions League appearances including games against Manchester City, Chelsea and Real Madrid. He made only a dozen appearances for Bayern before joining for Sunderland, but has since shown Wearsiders the quality associated with a player from one of the continent's very top clubs.

FULL NAME:
Jan Tilman Kirchhoff

POSITION:
Defensive midfield or centre-back

DATE OF BIRTH:
1 October 1990

PLACE OF BIRTH:
Frankfurt, Germany

SUNDERLAND DEBUT:
Tottenham Hotspur 4-1 Sunderland
16 January 2016

APPEARANCES:
14 (1)*

GOALS:
0*

*CORRECT AS OF 30.06.16

91

FULL NAME:
Steed Malbranque

POSITION:
Midfield

DATE OF BIRTH:
6 January 1980

PLACE OF BIRTH:
Mouscron, Belgium

SUNDERLAND DEBUT:
Sunderland 0-1 Liverpool
16 August 2008

APPEARANCES:
95 (17)

GOALS:
2

One of three players signed from Spurs in the summer of 2008 under Roy Keane, Steed Malbranque was a modern masterpiece.

A talented player with a low centre of gravity, excellent ball control, an eye for a pass and the ability to deliver it, Malbranque had caused Sunderland lots of problems in previous years in the white of both Tottenham and Fulham.

At Sunderland, he slotted seamlessly into the side playing all but two matches in his first season and managing to look a class act in a team that often struggled. He was a regular starter in the second of his three seasons, but in his last he became more peripheral. While named in the matchday squad for all 38 games, 14 of those were as a sub, albeit he only failed to get on three times, thereby making him second only to Jordan Henderson in first team appearances for the season.

While a regular goalscorer when in the capital, particularly at Craven Cottage, at Sunderland the goals dried up, Steed scoring only twice, one of them a cup goal against non-league Barrow. Nonetheless, Malbranque was always an entertaining player to watch.

Deemed surplus to requirements by Steve Bruce after Sunderland finished tenth in 2011, Malbranque returned to France with St. Etienne, before enjoying a second spell with

MALBRANQUE

Lyon with whom he had starred before coming into English football. In 2016 at the age of 36 he signed for Caen.

Resisting the opportunity to play for the country of his birth, Belgium, despite his undoubted ability Malbranque never won a full cap. He captained France at Under-18 level and played for les Bleus up to Under-21 level.

Johnny Mapson had the finest of 20th birthdays, waking up on his big day in the knowledge that 24 hours earlier he'd helped Sunderland to win the FA Cup for the first time.

He remained the youngest FA Cup final goalkeeper until 1969 when Peter Shilton kept goal for Leicester City, but as Leicester lost, Mapson remained the youngest goalkeeper to be on the winning side in the cup final.

Mapson had been at the club for just over a year. Signed shortly after the death of Jimmy Thorpe during the 1936 Championship winning campaign, Johnny had come in for the final seven games of that campaign and helped Sunderland seal the title.

Despite his youth, Mapson immediately made the goalkeeping position his own, missing just one match in each of his first two seasons in the north-east. Ever-present in the first post-war league season, he missed just a solitary game the year after.

In 1949/50 when Sunderland finished a point behind the champions he missed just the first two games (when just a point was taken) while in the following season Sunderland went into only one match minus Mapson. Making his 383rd and final appearance in March 1953 Johnny had amassed a substantial total, despite losing six seasons to the war.

Were it not for losing these seasons during his twenties, Mapson's total may well have rivalled the tally of 627 of record

MAPSON

holder Jim Montgomery, of course the only other 'keeper to win the cup with the club. Mapson's position in history is unique though as no-one else can match his achievement of keeping goal in Sunderland sides which won the league as well as the cup.

An excellent goalkeeper fully deserving of his place in the pantheon of SAFC 'keepers, Johnny Mapson played a war-time international for England and twice represented the FA on a tour of South Africa.

FULL NAME:
John Mapson

POSITION:
Goalkeeper

DATE OF BIRTH:
2 May 1917

PLACE OF BIRTH:
Birkenhead

SUNDERLAND DEBUT:
Sunderland 5-0 Portsmouth
4 April 1936

APPEARANCES:
383

FULL NAME:
James Millar

POSITION:
Forward

DATE OF BIRTH:
2 March 1870

PLACE OF BIRTH:
Annbank, Ayrshire

SUNDERLAND DEBUT:
Sunderland 2-3 Burnley
13 September 1890

APPEARANCES:
261

GOALS:
128

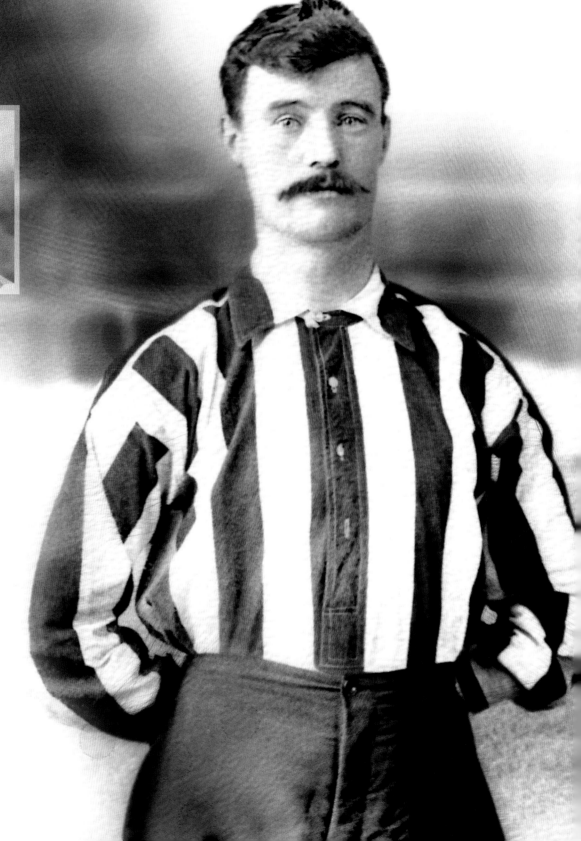

Debuting in Sunderland's first-ever league game, Millar scored twice in the club's first league victory. He also became the first of only four players in history to score five goals in a game for Sunderland and one of only two (with Ted Doig) to win four top-flight title medals with Sunderland.

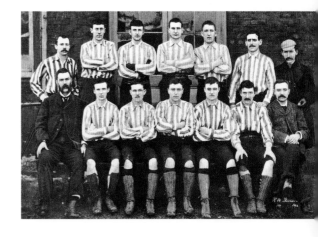

In between his third and fourth championship wins on Wearside, Millar went back to his native Scotland to play for Rangers where he won back-to-back Scottish titles at the turn of the century, meaning that in an eleven year spell from 1892 to 1902, he won six league championships.

In the first two of these as Sunderland became champions in 1892 and retained the title a year, later Millar played alongside his brother-in-law William Gibson. He also played in three Scottish Cup finals during his Ibrox sojourn, winning in 1897 and 1888. He represented the Scottish League three times and also won three Scotland caps while with Rangers but was never chosen when plying his trade south of the border.

A model of consistency, Millar missed only a dozen games amongst Sunderland's first four title winning campaigns. A skilful player, Jamie was two-footed and had tremendous ball control. His five-goal haul came in Sunderland's record 11-1 victory over Fairfield in the English (F.A.) Cup in February 1895, while he also scored ten hat-tricks for the Lads.

JAMIE MILLAR

After leaving Sunderland in 1904, he served West Bromwich Albion and Chelsea as trainer, making one league appearance for WBA in October 1904.

Sadly this Sunderland great died from tuberculosis a month before what would have been his 37th birthday.

FULL NAME:
James Montgomery

POSITION:
Goalkeeper

DATE OF BIRTH:
9 October 1943

PLACE OF BIRTH:
Sunderland

SUNDERLAND DEBUT:
Sunderland 5-2 Walsall
4 October 1961

APPEARANCES:
627

Sunderland's record appearance maker, with 169 more games played than anyone else, Jim Montgomery sometimes jokes that people just remember two.

One of those of course is the 1973 FA Cup final, when his legendary double-save from Leeds' Trevor Cherry and Peter Lorimer became renowned as the greatest save ever made at the national stadium, resulting in worldwide fame for 'the Mighty Jim'. The other game Monty refers to came in the same competition nine years earlier, a quarter-final replay at home to Manchester United. On that occasion his scuffed kick went straight to Denis Law, who scored.

Jim feels that the way the crowd responded to lift him after that mistake showed how much they were with him, giving him great belief. Monty had fully earned that respect and continued to deserve it. In 2016 when he was awarded the Freedom of Sunderland; to add to the British Empire Medal he'd received the year before, it was a token from the city that as well as being a huge footballing hero, Monty holds the immense respect of everyone on Wearside.

As a modern-day ambassador of the club, Jim has probably attended more functions than he played games. During these he has proved himself as good off the pitch as he was on it, which is saying something. Never egotistical or self-centred, Jim's ability to engage with supporters is indicative of the connection established between the team and the terraces when he played.

JIMMY MONTGOMERY

As a goalkeeper 'Monty' was brilliant. The rest of the world were astonished by his Wembley wonder-save but Sunderland supporters weren't even surprised. Seemingly impossible reaction saves of great agility were Jim's stock in trade. He did it week in, week out. Those in the know will tell you the best of his games wasn't against Leeds, but at Leeds Road, where Sunderland played Huddersfield in December 1962.

By the time of his Huddersfield heroics, Monty was still in his teens and on his way to his first ever-present season having broken into the side in the previous year.
He would play every match in the following campaign too as he helped Sunderland to their first-ever promotion.

Injury, change of management and the subsequent signing of Sandy McLaughlan meant that Monty was more out of the team, than in for the next 18 months, but having been restored for a home game with Newcastle at the start of 1966, he didn't miss a match for two years.

By now though he was maturing as a goalkeeper and wasn't just the number one at Sunderland, he was one of the best in the country, winning England Under-23 honours and making the full squad. From 3 January 1966 to just before Christmas 1972, Monty missed just four matches. In the cup-winning season of 1972/73, the only game he missed was on the Monday before the final when he was rested ahead of the show-piece occasion.

It took Sunderland three years to win promotion after winning the cup, but Jim missed just five games in that time before promotion was secured. Amazingly, despite starting with back-to-back clean sheets in the top flight, Monty was to play just four more league games for the Lads. Bob Stokoe's signing of Barry Siddall from Bolton resulted in Jim's final appearance coming in a 1-0 League Cup defeat at Manchester United 15 years and two days after his debut.

MONTGOMERY

Monty was three days short of his 33rd birthday. He went on to play for Southampton on loan, Birmingham City and Brian Clough's Nottingham Forest, with whom he won a European Cup medal as an unused sub.

In 1980, Jim returned to Roker as player/coach, but never made another first-team appearance.

FULL NAME:
James Montgomery

POSITION:
Goalkeeper

DATE OF BIRTH:
9 October 1943

PLACE OF BIRTH:
Sunderland

SUNDERLAND DEBUT:
Sunderland 5-2 Walsall
4 October 1961

APPEARANCES:
627

FULL NAME:
Ibrahim Ndong

POSITION:
Central midfield

DATE OF BIRTH:
17 June 1994

PLACE OF BIRTH:
Lambarene, Gabon

SUNDERLAND DEBUT:
Sunderland 0-3 Everton
12 September 2016

APPEARANCES:
4

GOALS:
0*

***CORRECT
AS OF 14.10.16**

Masterpieces start as a blank canvas. In choosing to include Didier Ndong as one of the players featured in this book, the hope is that the man who commanded Sunderland's record up-front fee of £13.5m, when he signed just as the transfer window closed on 31 August 2016, will live up to his billing and be a modern work of art in the way that some of the bygone players in this book can be seen as old masters.

Ndong certainly arrived with a big reputation, commanding that big fee just a couple of months after turning 22. Having come to prominence in Tunisian football, spending four years with CS Sfaxion, he moved to France with Lorient in January 2015, by which time he had already become a full international with the West African country of Gabon, for whom he debuted in June 2013.

Sent off on his first start in France and also in his final Ligue 1 appearance, Ndong certainly likes a tackle. If Picasso had his blue period, Didier has certainly had his yellow as well as his red ones, as yellow cards have frequently come the way of the mobile midfielder.

Cautions are inevitable for someone whose job it is to win the ball, but unlike so many ball-winners Ndong can also use it once he has possession.

NDONG

In his one full season in Ligue 1 he achieved an impressive 87.3% pass completion rate and while not a regular goalscorer, has shown he has the ability to whack a shot into the top corner from way outside the box.

If he can do that at Sunderland and help control the midfield, Didier may well become a player who supporters come to see as a work of art in his own right ...and not just for his hairstyle!

FULL NAME:
Kevin Phillips

POSITION:
Striker

DATE OF BIRTH:
25 July 1973

PLACE OF BIRTH:
Hitchin

SUNDERLAND DEBUT:
Sunderland 3-1 Manchester City
15 August 1997

APPEARANCES:
233 (2)

GOALS:
130

The last time Sunderland had the country's top striker was when Kevin Phillips was at his peak. SuperKev became the only Englishman to win the Adidas Golden Shoe when he struck 30 Premier League goals in 1999/2000.

In total, Phillips tucked away a further century of goals for the red and whites. Not only does this make him one of only three players to top a ton for Sunderland since the second World War, but Phillips is way out in front as the club's record post-war marksman.

The classic 'fox in the box' Kevin was never static, his 'Phil-osophy' being to always be on the move in the box. He was blessed by being on the same wavelength as Niall Quinn and Quinn's radar enabled him to frequently find SuperKev.

Dubbed the 'Hitchin Hot-shot' by the late Ian Laws, another of Phillips' mantras was 'never be afraid to miss'. Phillips missed plenty of chances and wasn't in Gary Rowell's league when it came to converting penalties, but another of Kevin's attributes was that unlike some strikers who might hide if they've missed a good opportunity, Phillips wouldn't bat an eyelid, he'd just be in the right place at the right time next time too. If he was buying a raffle ticket with every run, sooner or later Phillips would find he had the winning number.

Decent in the air and not shy to take a shot with his left foot, it was Phillips' right peg that inflicted most damage on opponents.

KEVIN PHILLIPS

Although SuperKev was primarily a penalty box poacher, the goal that became his trademark was one which would see him cut in from the inside left position and curl a right footer into the top corner from the edge of the box.

Two of SuperKev's finest goals came in his most productive season as he fired newly promoted Sunderland to their highest league placing in since 1955 when they finished seventh in millennium year.

Local rivals Newcastle had been by far the dominant of the north-east sides in recent years when Peter Reid's red and whites turned up at St. James' on a night of torrential rain.

Sunderland famously came from behind to win, Phillips getting the winner with a typical piece of opportunism. He'd seen a good chance saved - but never being afraid to miss - was first to the rebound and spun to chip the 'keeper with a piece of sheer brilliance.

It was a moment and a result that gave Sunderland real belief. The next away game in the Premier League saw SuperKev score a hat-trick as Sunderland won 5-0 at Derby and the goals just kept coming. When Chelsea came north before Christmas Phillips and Quinn scored twice each in another big win, a screamer from SuperKev being one of his best ever.

Going on to reach 30 goals that season, it was the second time in three seasons Phillips had topped that figure. Kevin's first season had seen him mark his debut with a goal in the Stadium of Light's first-ever league game and go on to break Brian Clough's post-war scoring record. SuperKev achieved that at Wembley with his 35th goal of the campaign in the 1998 Play-Off final. The promotion season saw him top-score with a more modest 23 league goals, these from just 26 games in an injury-hit season.

PHILLIPS

Playing on until he was almost 41, Phillips ended up with a tally of 282 goals in 660 games in all competitions. In a well-travelled career, he also won promotion with WBA, Birmingham City, Crystal Palace (for whom he hit the winner in the Play-Off final against former employers Watford) and finally Leicester, where his debut saw him come on as sub for Jamie Vardy. The fox in the box then moved into coaching with the Foxes ...where no doubt Vardy learned from England international SuperKev.

FULL NAME:
Kevin Phillips

POSITION:
Striker

DATE OF BIRTH:
25 July 1973

PLACE OF BIRTH:
Hitchin

SUNDERLAND DEBUT:
Sunderland 3-1 Manchester City
15 August 1997

APPEARANCES:
233 (2)

GOALS:
130

FULL NAME:
John (Ian) Porterfield

POSITION:
Midfield

DATE OF BIRTH:
11 February 1946

PLACE OF BIRTH:
Dunfermline

SUNDERLAND DEBUT:
Sunderland 3-3 Newcastle United
30 December 1967

APPEARANCES:
256 (12)

GOALS:
19

Ian Porterfield was tall, gangly and never the quickest. He could play though. In recent years the player most like him was Jordi Gomez, albeit Porter was a much better player than the Spanish schemer.

Porterfield was never hurried, while the pace of the game around him could be frenetic, Ian eased through games, his mind was always one step ahead and his speed was in his brain, where he could see a pass early and deliver a telling ball.

He earned worldwide fame for scoring the only goal of the 1973 FA Cup final. Just as ironically, as a maker of goals being famed as a taker of them, Ian's iconic strike was hit with his right foot when he was almost entirely left footed. Indeed, in those days the scorer of the winning goal in the cup final was presented with a golden boot and Porterfield requested that he received a left-footed boot rather than the right-footed one with which he hit his Wembley winner.

Porterfield hailed from the same part of Scotland as Jim Baxter and like Baxter, had made his name with Raith Rovers. Baxter was the better player, world class in fact, but Porterfield was the more useful servant to Sunderland, quite apart from his cup final heroics.

Porterfield painted masterpieces in his creative role at Roker Park. Baxter had liked to call his left foot, 'The claw', but Porterfield's boot - golden or otherwise - could be claw-like too. Frequently he would raise his left foot, almost Inspector Gadget-like and simply control a high ball as easily as if he was picking an apple off a tree.

PORTERFIELD

With the ball under his spell, 'Porter' could pick a pass and set Sunderland on their way.

Later he managed all over the world at club and international level, that cup final winner always impressing on the CV, but make no mistake about it, Ian Porterfield was a terrific player for the Lads with or without the cherry on the top of that magical moment against Leeds.

Centre-forward, manager, chairman, director for international development, even goalkeeper, Niall Quinn did it all.

It was Niall who pulled together the Drumaville Consortium to buy the club when it was at a very low ebb after a particularly desperate relegation with 15 points in 2006. The famous Quinn quote, "I learned my trade at Arsenal, became a footballer at Manchester City, but Sunderland got under my skin" went a long way to explaining why the Republic of Ireland international eschewed the golf course, the pundits perch and the pub (No not the pub) in order to come back to the club he loves and drag it back to the top flight.

Niall knew Sunderland needed an injection of charisma, a sprinkling of stardust, and having taken over as the front-man of the new owners, he took on the manager's role himself while he waited for a box office name to take over, eventually tempting Roy Keane into his first managerial position.

As good a front-man off the pitch as he was on it, Quinn stayed until Sunderland were in the top half of the top flight and through to the quarter-final of the FA Cup before leaving the stage.

Good times were what Sunderland were used to when Quinn was a player. A record £1.3m fee was paid for him by his ex-Manchester City manager Peter Reid and after debuting

QUINN

in Sunderland's first Premier League game, Niall scored twice on his full debut.

Teaming up with Kevin Phillips a year later, Niall got the first goal and the first hat-trick at the Stadium of Light, and as a talismanic target-man helped turn his previously unknown strike partner into SuperKev.

A giant in every respect, Niall Quinn is the biggest and most important figure in the club's Stadium of Light era.

FULL NAME:
Niall John Quinn

POSITION:
Centre-forward

DATE OF BIRTH:
6 October 1966

PLACE OF BIRTH:
Dublin

SUNDERLAND DEBUT:
Sunderland 0-0 Leicester City
17 August 1996

APPEARANCES:
183 (37)

GOALS:
69

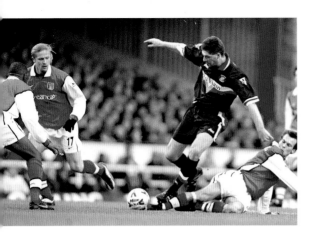

In the fabulous early years at the Stadium of Light, Quinny was the fulcrum of the side. SuperKev grabbed most of the goals and the headlines that went with them, but it was Quinn the team revolved around.

Wingers Nicky Summerbee and Allan 'Magic' Johnston each had superb understandings with their respective full-backs, Chris Makin and Mickey Gray. Consequently, the supply line was as productive as nearby Nissan, and with Quinn as their target, they had enormous success.

As good a target-man as there has been in the game, Quinn was unquestionably the jewel of the Niall. Not only was he fantastic in the air, but he had an adhesive touch if the ball was fired into his feet, while even a ball pinged at his chest or thighs would still find the Irishman able to hold it up or lay it off into the path of Phillips, who simply kept finding the net.

Describing his attributes as a footballer doesn't do Niall justice. He was, and is, as brilliant off the pitch as he was on it. What you saw was what you got with Niall. He was as genuine as your best mate. Whether talking to visiting royalty or someone who had just staggered out of 'The Royalty' Niall treated everyone equally, and that respect earned him the same back in droves.

QUINN

Factor in the donation of the £1m earned from his Benefit Match to fund children's hospitals in Sunderland and Dublin, not to mention the 'These are my people' comment, before he organised and paid for taxis back to Sunderland from Bristol Airport; when airline staff refused to take off with a plane full of boisterously happy Sunderland supporters, and you realise that the famed Magic Carpet of Niall Quinn was one heck of a ride.

FULL NAME:
Niall John Quinn

POSITION:
Centre-forward

DATE OF BIRTH:
6 October 1966

PLACE OF BIRTH:
Dublin

SUNDERLAND DEBUT:
Sunderland 0-0 Leicester City
17 August 1996

APPEARANCES:
183 (37)

GOALS:
69

Without doubt the greatest character to ever play for Sunderland - and arguably any club! L.R. Roose was a goalkeeper who forced the Football Association to change the Laws of the game.

Until 1910, goalies could handle the ball anywhere on the pitch. For many this was a technicality as they didn't venture far from home. Not Roose! He liked to bounce the ball to almost the half-way line and then launch it one handed into the opposition box for his only too willing forwards.

In an age before celebrity, L.R. Roose was a celebrity. Known to have a woman in every town, and often more than one, he had a high-profile relationship with the massively famous Music Hall performer Marie Lloyd. Coming from an ecclesiastical family, Roose was nicknamed the Archdeacon. He also liked to pass himself off as a doctor, although he never qualified. He did though, work in a London hospital and liked to play as an amateur. This enabled him to be paid expenses only and boy did he wrack up the expenses, making outrageous demands on his clubs who paid up because he was such a good goalkeeper.

He virtually bankrupted Stoke who he played for before joining SAFC - despite the fact he'd previously punched a Sunderland supporter. The Wearside crowd loved him though and presented him with an 'Illuminated Address' in praise of his abilities after his final game in which he broke his arm against Newcastle.

ROOSE

Always a practical joker, Wales international Roose once turned up for a game with Ireland with his arm bandaged, only to discard the bandage just before kick–off admitting there was nothing wrong with him.

Taught by the author of 'The War of the Worlds' HG Wells, sadly L.R. Roose was killed in action at the Battle of the Somme in World War One.

FULL NAME:
Leigh Richmond Roose

POSITION:
Goalkeeper

DATE OF BIRTH:
26 November 1877

PLACE OF BIRTH:
Holt, near Wrexham

SUNDERLAND DEBUT:
Preston North End 3-2 Sunderland
18 January 1908

APPEARANCES:
99

Of all the players to have played for Sunderland, there can be few, if any who were or are bigger Sunderland supporters than Gary Rowell.

Still in 2016 as this book is written, Gary is at every home game without fail and still 'kicks every ball,' while afterwards his own personal post-mortem is as heart-felt as that of any fan. Gary was a supporter before he came through the ranks at Roker Park, witnessed the FA Cup triumph of 1973 from the vantage point of being a youth teamer and at one point bunked off training in order to attend a game during the cup run, desperately hoping that Bob Stokoe didn't find out. It was appropriate then that when Rowell debuted as a sub just before Christmas in 1975, the score in his first match was 1-0 with the scorer being Ian Porterfield.

While Gary remains in awe of the 'Team of '73' he duly became a bona-fide hero himself. Now over three decades after he left the club, the Red and White army still sing of 'Living in a Gary Rowell World' - Rowell's name being sung more regularly than any other former player. And why not? After all, Gary is the man who scored a hat-trick away to Newcastle, is one of only three players to score a century of goals for the club since World War Two, notched a top-flight hat-trick against Arsenal and to date is the last Sunderland player to score a winning goal away to Liverpool.

ROWELL

Many of Gary's goals came while he was playing in midfield. He was the master of ghosting into the box unnoticed and had the knack of being in the right place at the right time.

A lot of his goals were scored from close range where he made goalscoring look easy, his natural ability to read the game allowed him to regularly be the 'Johnny on the spot.'

FULL NAME:
Gary Rowell

POSITION:
Midfield/striker

DATE OF BIRTH:
6 June 1957

PLACE OF BIRTH:
Seaham

SUNDERLAND DEBUT:
Sunderland 1-0 Oxford United
13 December 1975

APPEARANCES:
269 (28)

GOALS:
101

FULL NAME:
Gary Rowell

POSITION:
Midfield/striker

DATE OF BIRTH:
6 June 1957

PLACE OF BIRTH:
Seaham

SUNDERLAND DEBUT:
Sunderland 1-0 Oxford United
13 December 1975

APPEARANCES:
269 (28)

GOALS:
101

Another of Gary's great attributes was his brilliant penalty taking. He scored 21 out of the 22 he took, slotting them right into the corners. Often the 'keeper went the wrong way, but even if the stopper guessed right Rowell's placement was such that even the best goalies couldn't get anywhere near.

Rowell was part of a trophy-winning side under Bob Stokoe. He made three starts as well as his debut as a sub in the Second Division Championship winning side of 1976, his first goal coming in a big and important late-season victory at Hull. Gary began to establish himself in the starting line-up in the top flight the following season, particularly after the appointment of Jimmy Adamson as manager, when along with fellow youngsters Kevin Arnott and Shaun Elliott, he provided youthful dynamism in a previously struggling side. When the tide turned and Sunderland hit form, the teenager suddenly scored four goals in three games as his bottom of the league side successively produced 4-0, 6-1 and 6-0 wins.

It wasn't enough to prevent relegation, but by now Gary was a key member of the side and was capped by England at U21 level. The following season was the first of six seasons out of seven where he was top-scorer (Joint top in all competitions in the last of those, 1983/84). The odd year out in that run Gary's only goal was an early-season Anglo-Scottish Cup penalty in a season where he fought back from serious injury.

ROWELL

Surprisingly released in the summer of 1984, Rowell joined Norwich and later continued his career with 'Boro, Brighton, Carlisle and Burnley. In the season after he left Sunderland he found himself ruled out by injury, when his new club met his old one in the League Cup final at Wembley. While this time, 1-0 was the score Sunderland lost by at Wembley, Canary Gary took the trophy and held it aloft to the Sunderland fans who still idolised him - and still do.

FULL NAME:
Leonard Francis Shackleton

POSITION:
Inside-forward

DATE OF BIRTH:
3 May 1922

PLACE OF BIRTH:
Bradford

SUNDERLAND DEBUT:
Derby County 5-1 Sunderland
14 February 1948

APPEARANCES:
348

GOALS:
100

Probably more than any other player in the club's history, 'Shack' put people on the gate. His talent for entertaining was irresistible, he was the maverick's maverick.

By reading this book you are almost certainly a Sunderland supporter and if you aren't old enough to have seen him - and as his final appearance was in 1957, you'd be getting on a bit - then you'll have no doubt heard all about 'The Clown Prince of Soccer.'

It's true that 'Shack' could play a one-two off the corner flag (In at least one game he did it twice), it's true that he could put back-spin on even the leather 'casey's' of his era so that he tempted opponents to lunge for the ball only for it to spin back to the 'Clown Prince', it's true that as he didn't get on with centre-forward Trevor Ford. He would often play passes to him which were just too long or short whereas passes to other teammates were inch perfect.

It's also true that some of his best performances were reserved for games against Arsenal, who had rejected him as a boy, and his former team Newcastle, Shack famously observing, "I'm not biased when it comes to Newcastle, I'm not bothered who beats them."

LEN
SHACKLETON

It's also true that one of his off the pitch party-pieces was to flick a coin from his foot into his blazer pocket and it's true that in 1954 he scored a goal of mesmerizing skill for England against the reigning world champions West Germany - and was never picked again.

FULL NAME:
Leonard Francis Shackleton

POSITION:
Inside-forward

DATE OF BIRTH:
3 May 1922

PLACE OF BIRTH:
Bradford

SUNDERLAND DEBUT:
Derby County 5-1 Sunderland
14 February 1948

APPEARANCES:
348

GOALS:
100

That seems harsh, but for figures in authority the 'clown' part of his nickname irritated more than the 'Prince of football' impressed, no matter how good he was. This after all, was the man who in his autobiography really did entitle a chapter, 'The average director's knowledge of football' ...and left the page blank!

'Shack' could be unplayable. He could be brilliant and then some. Hardly surprisingly supporters absolutely loved him. Bill Shankly summed up the balance you need in a football team by reckoning you need eight people to 'carry the piano' and three to play it.

Len didn't need anyone to help him tickle the ivories, he could be the maestro all on his own. Football supporters love a trier and rightly so, but when they pay their money to pass through the turnstile they want to see someone do what they can't do with a football - and Shack couldn't just make the ball talk - he could tell it what to say.

Three decades before Skinner & Baddiel came up with 'Fantasy Football' Shack was playing it. He scored six goals on his Newcastle debut, but lost 5-1 on his first Sunderland appearance. He's still admired on Tyneside, but he's idolised on Wearside.

LEN SHACKLETON

Only Gary Rowell and Kevin Phillips have emulated Shack in scoring 100 goals for Sunderland since World War Two, but if facts and figures fail to tell the tale of any player, it's The Clown Prince of Soccer, as there was only one Len Shackleton.

Dubbed the 'Son of Pele' by fans, Martin Smith always had a touch of class. A pupil of Monkwearmouth School - just across the fence from where the club's training ground now stands - in 1990, Smith had been a key part of the Sunderland Schools side that reached the final of the FA Schools Trophy.

As red and white as they come, Martin chose to sign for his local side ahead of a host of clubs including Manchester United and Arsenal. His first-team debut was as eagerly awaited and when it arrived he didn't disappoint, the 18-year-old scoring with a free kick at the Fulwell End.

Possessing plenty of ability and pace befitting a schoolboy 200m champion, Smithy could torment full-backs and finished his first season with a healthy nine goals from 33 games in a side that saw a change of manager (from Terry Butcher to Mick Buxton) shortly after he got into the team. It would be the next manager for whom Martin would play a key role. Peter Reid was appointed with seven games to go of Smith's first full season. The youngster scored in the last three, the first of those a crucial winner in a key game against Swindon Town.

Although Martin won a championship medal in 1995/96, he missed most of the season and played only sporadically from then until his release in 1999. Signing for Sheffield United, who the 'Son of Pele' pointed out, 'at least play in red and white stripes' in his first season Martin scored in a cup-tie at Newcastle.

SMITH

He had been jeered at St. James' as a Sunderland player on his England U21 debut and although he scored for the Blades, was taunted 'Mackem, what's the score?' as his side trailed 4-1. Never lost for an answer, Smith held up his hands to signal 2-1, Sunderland having won by that score at Newcastle earlier in the season.

You can take the boy out of Sunderland but you can't take Sunderland out of the boy!

FULL NAME:
Martin Geoffrey Smith

POSITION:
Midfield/forward

DATE OF BIRTH:
13 November 1974

PLACE OF BIRTH:
Sunderland

SUNDERLAND DEBUT:
Sunderland 2-0 Luton Town
20 October 1993

APPEARANCES:
107 (38)

GOALS:
28

Nicky Summerbee was a marvellously effective winger. The main aim of the position is to be a supply line and Summerbee was a superb crosser of the ball.

Unlike Allan 'Magic' Johnston who was on the opposite flank during Summerbee's best times at Sunderland, Nicky wasn't the sort of winger who liked to leave his marker looking like someone who had enthusiastically lost at 'Twister', Summerbee simply wanted to work half-a-yard of space and then whip over an inviting cross. Fortunately for Nicky, the man receiving most of these invitations was Niall Quinn, who usually ended up bringing Super-Kevin Phillips to the party.

Summerbee's dad Mike, had been a brilliant right-winger in his day for Manchester City and England, while Nick's Grandad George had made over 150 league appearances, beginning at Aldershot alongside his brother - and Nick's Great Uncle - Gordon.

Signing for Peter Reid in an exchange deal with Craig Russell, Summerbee was valued at £1m and proved to be an astute capture. Combining brilliantly with right-back Chris Makin, Nick was part of the record-breaking 105 point promotion-winning side of 1999. A year earlier he had scored at Wembley in the Play-Off final with Charlton, also netting in the ill-fated penalty shoot out.

SUMMERBEE

Summerbee would spend a third season on Wearside playing regularly in the Premiership as he helped Sunderland to the first of the back-to-back seventh placed finishes under Reid. Nick's time at the Stadium of Light can be summed up in a single word: quality.

FULL NAME:
Nicholas John Summerbee

POSITION:
Right-winger

DATE OF BIRTH:
26 August 1971

PLACE OF BIRTH:
Altrincham

SUNDERLAND DEBUT:
Portsmouth 1-4 Sunderland
15 November 1997

APPEARANCES:
100 (8)

GOALS:
8

Known as 'Toddy' later in his career; indeed that was the title of his biography, Colin was always 'Toddo' at Sunderland. The chant 'T.O.D.D.O. - Toddo' frequently rang out when he played at Roker Park, while a glance at the contents page of the best selling 'All the Lads' book shows an iconic piece of Toddo graffiti!

Another popular Todd terrace ditty promised that the national side were off to the 1970 Mexico World Cup, 'With Colin Todd in the England squad,' but while the then 21-year-old made Sir Alf Ramsay's initial squad of 40, he missed out on the final cut.

In fact Toddo wouldn't make his full England debut until 15 months after leaving Sunderland, by which time he'd won a League title medal with Derby in 1972. He'd won the first of his 14 Under-23 caps when still a teenager against Hungary in May 1968 at Everton's Goodison Park, a ground he would later call home.

Colin Todd was a player of genuine class. He was a first class reader of the game, possessed terrific vision, was swift in covering the ground and could deliver telling, immaculately-weighted passes. One example a week before his 22nd birthday in December 1970 encapsulated Colin's class. Defending the Roker End, Toddo broke up a Queens Park Rangers attack on the edge of the box and broke to the half way line before spraying an inch-perfect ball out to the left flank where Gordon Harris took up the invitation to counter attack and provide a terrific cross which Billy Hughes headed home for a superb goal.

TODD

Todd was just 17 when he debuted in the top flight less than six weeks after England won the World Cup in 1966.

He ended the season having been a mainstay as Sunderland won the FA Youth Cup, while at first-team level, he played in over half the games and was ever-present a season later missing just one game the following campaign.

FULL NAME:
Colin Todd

POSITION:
Defender

DATE OF BIRTH:
12 December 1948

PLACE OF BIRTH:
Chester-le-Street

SUNDERLAND DEBUT:
Chelsea 1-1 Sunderland
10 September 1966

APPEARANCES:
188 (3)

GOALS:
3

FULL NAME:
Colin Todd

POSITION:
Defender

DATE OF BIRTH:
12 December 1948

PLACE OF BIRTH:
Chester-le-Street

SUNDERLAND DEBUT:
Chelsea 1-1 Sunderland
10 September 1966

APPEARANCES:
188 (3)

GOALS:
3

He was certainly missed as the club's record defeat of 0-8 was equalled at West Ham in his absence.

Colin's consistency would continue in 1969/70 as he missed just two games, but he was excelling in a struggling side as Sunderland were relegated. Todd would miss just two of the first 28 games of the following season, the last being in a 4-0 home defeat at the hands of Cardiff City, which left Sunderland 12th in the second tier the day before Valentine's Day. He had missed just five games in three-and-a-half seasons when Sunderland accepted a record transfer fee of £170,00 for a defender in February 1971.

The purchasing manager was none other than former Sunderland player and youth coach Brian Clough, who took him to high-flying Derby. Colin played 40 of the 42 league games as the Rams became champions in 1972 and missed just three, when the title was won again in 1975, when he was named PFA Player of the Year.

In September 1978, Todd moved to Everton for £330,000, joining Birmingham for £30,000 less than a year later, duly helping Blues to promotion. A further link-up with Clough at Forest followed before as a veteran he helped Oxford to the third division title in 1984 and having a spell with Vancouver Whitecaps before signing-off as a player with two games for Luton in November 1984, taking his career league total to 668.

COLIN TODD

His boots hung up, Colin began an extensive career in management which took him from a first job at Whitley Bay to an extensive stint in Denmark with Randers up to 2016, by way of Middlesbrough, Bolton, Swindon, Derby, Bradford City, Randers, Darlington and Randers again. At the end of the 2015/16 season Colin had managed in 677 competitive fixtures.

FULL NAME:
Mark Anthony Towers

POSITION:
Midfield

DATE OF BIRTH:
13 April 1952

PLACE OF BIRTH:
Manchester

SUNDERLAND DEBUT:
Sunderland 1-0 Fulham
16 March 1974

APPEARANCES:
124

GOALS:
22

Ruling the midfield with the authority of an emperor, Towers won three England caps in the month after helping Sunderland to the Division Two title in 1976.

He had both scored and been sent off against Sunderland during the Lads' run to FA Cup glory in 1973, while with Manchester City, with whom he had won the European Cup Winners' Cup when still a teenager in 1970. Although Sunderland spiked City's Wembley ambitions in 1973, Tony played for City beneath the twin towers in the 1974 League Cup final (losing to Wolves) just a fortnight before his debut for Sunderland.

Bob Stokoe took Tony as part of a deal which saw two of the team of '73; Mick Horswill and Dennis Tueart, move to the blue half of Manchester. Although Sunderland won six of Towers' first eight games in the closing stages of the season, they finished three points off Luton in the second and final promotion place, Tony scoring in the final fixture away to the already promoted Hatters who were defeated in a seven-goal thriller.

Sunderland narrowly missed out on promotion in Towers' first full season, but made no mistake the following year when with strikers Pop Robson and Mel Holden scoring 13 and 12 goals respectively, Tony was third top scorer with ten, half of these

TONY
TOWERS

coming from the penalty spot, including one on the day promotion was secured against Bolton.

A year later, Towers moved on to Birmingham City following a change of manager (to Jimmy Adamson) and relegation. Tony continued his playing days in America and Canada before signing off with two brief appearances for Rochdale in 1985 under the management of his former Sunderland teammate Vic Halom.

FULL NAME:
Dennis Tueart

POSITION:
Left-winger

DATE OF BIRTH:
29 November 1949

PLACE OF BIRTH:
Newcastle

SUNDERLAND DEBUT:
Sunderland 0-0 Sheffield Wednesday
26 December 1968

APPEARANCES:
208 (6)

GOALS:
56

Whenever Dennis Tueart got the ball, the level of expectation rose in the crowd. He was such an exciting player and had a brilliant career after beginning at Sunderland where he was a key member of the 1973 FA Cup winning side.

Three years later, when with Manchester City, he scored at Wembley against his hometown team Newcastle with a brilliant bicycle-kick in the League Cup final. Such was his ability to excite that New York Cosmos signed him to replace Pele, Tueart taking to the game stateside with the gusto that typified him. Dennis deserved to win many more than his eight caps for England and after his playing days, served Manchester City as an energetic and effective director. Always cute commercially, his outstanding autobiography 'My Football Journey' was produced in both Sunderland and Manchester City cover versions, Dennis donating the proceeds to the Christie cancer centre in Manchester.

Dennis debuted on Boxing Day 1968. He had a tough man to dislodge in Scotland international George Mulhall, who came on for Dennis on Tueart's debut. The youngster got another chance in March - scoring when given the full 90 minutes - and a further month on, was brought into the side for the final eight games of the season.

Having shown what he could do, Tueart missed just a three game run the following season. He couldn't prevent Sunderland going down, but did notch the winner at Maine Road where so many of his goals would be scored in years to come.

TUEART

At the start of the following 1970/71 campaign, Tueart was left out by manager Alan 'Bomber' Brown. It was the eighth game of the season when he was brought off the bench with Sunderland a goal down at home to Brown's former club Sheffield Wednesday. Tueart was like a man possessed as he showed the scintillating pace and directness that was to make him such a handful for even the best defences. Sunderland roared back to win 3-1, Tueart capping his impact with the final goal.

FULL NAME:
Dennis Tueart

POSITION:
Left-winger

DATE OF BIRTH:
29 November 1949

PLACE OF BIRTH:
Newcastle

SUNDERLAND DEBUT:
Sunderland 0-0 Sheffield Wednesday
26 December 1968

APPEARANCES:
208 (6)

GOALS:
56

In 1971/72 Dennis played in every game, starting all but the opening two games, when he came off the bench. He was joint top league goal-scorer with Dave Watson with 13 apiece, and got another couple in cup-ties.

In the glorious cup-winning season of 1972/73 Tueart was rested ahead of the final and quarter-final, but started every other match, netting a dozen in the league and three in the cup. Along with Billy Hughes on the opposite flank, the pair terrorised every team put in their way.

Both scored in the first away game of the following season as the cup-holders looked like they'd walk the league, winning 4-1 at Notts County, where the cup run had begun. That didn't prove to be the case as teams raised their game against Bob Stokoe's side, but Tueart was in the form of his life. In mid-September, he scored a third-minute winner at Oxford with a scissor kick every bit as spectacular as the bicycle-kick he'd demonstrate to a wider audience at Wembley in 1976. Four days after his 'Lord of the Manor Ground' goal, he scored an even better one in Sunderland's first-ever European game.

Against Vasas Budapest, in Hungary, Tueart picked up the ball near the half-way line and proceeded to slalom through the home defence before finishing clinically. It was a top-class goal from a player who by now was absolutely brilliant and desperate to play at the highest level. He soon added a Roker Park hat-trick in the league, but come March - ten months to the day since winning

TUEART

at Wembley with Sunderland - Dennis's brace in a 3-0 home win still only saw Stokoe's side tenth in the table. It proved to be Tueart's final appearance for Sunderland. He left for Manchester City, and was called up by England for the first time on the same day!

Dennis scored over 100 goals for City, for whom he also played in the 1981 FA Cup final, and played briefly for Stoke and Burnley before hanging up his boots in 1984.

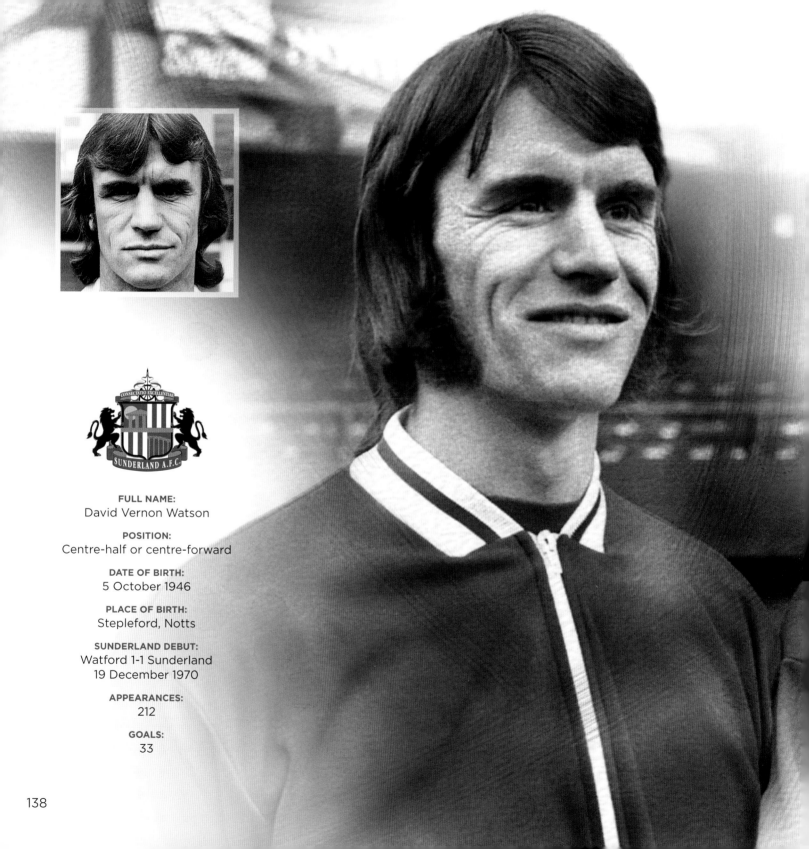

FULL NAME:
David Vernon Watson

POSITION:
Centre-half or centre-forward

DATE OF BIRTH:
5 October 1946

PLACE OF BIRTH:
Stepleford, Notts

SUNDERLAND DEBUT:
Watford 1-1 Sunderland
19 December 1970

APPEARANCES:
212

GOALS:
33

No-one surpasses the 14 England caps won as a Sunderland player by Dave Watson, who rose to fame as the Man of the Match in the 1973 FA Cup final.

Originally a centre-half, signed by Sunderland as a centre-forward and converted back to centre-half, Watson went on to win 65 caps in a career that took him to Manchester City, Werder Bremen (Germany), Southampton, Stoke City, Vancouver Whitecaps (Canada), Derby County, Fort Lauderdale (USA), back to his first club Notts County as player/coach in 1984 and finally Kettering Town a year later.

When joining Sunderland from Rotherham United in December 1970, manager Alan Brown paid Sunderland's first £100,000 fee for a player he viewed as a centre-forward. Brown had been a centre-half himself, but was impressed by Watson's prowess in the opposition's box. In the first half of the 1970/71 season, he'd scored nine goals in 18 third division (now League One) appearances for the Millers including a hat-trick against Rochdale, benefitting from the crossing of Neil Warnock, who went on to a colourful career in management.

Brown was right, Watson was a very good centre-forward, but when Brown left, caretaker manager Billy Elliott switched him back to centre-half where Watson proved to be a truly great player. Nonetheless, Dave made a scoring debut for Sunderland as a striker where he took over from veteran England international Joe Baker. Watson found the back of the net again on his second home appearance against Carlisle in what was his only goal at

WATSON

Roker Park in his first season, where he finished with a meagre four goals in 17 games.

That goal-scoring appearance against Carlisle was Watson's fourth and final game alongside Colin Todd in a Sunderland shirt. What a partnership they could have been at Roker Park. The pair later played together for England on 13 of the 14 appearances Watson played for his country while on SAFC's books. In total 20 of Todd's 27 caps were won with Watson as a teammate.

Following Todd's departure from Wearside, Watson's first full season saw him score in an opening day home draw with Birmingham.

That 1971/72 season saw Dave play every one of the 51 games played in League and cup. He was top scorer with 15 goals, 13 of them in the league plus goals in the FA and Anglo-Italian cups.

Despite Anglo-Italian fixtures, major European football seemed a million miles away when Sunderland kicked off the 1972/73 campaign, when of course Sunderland won the FA Cup to qualify for the European Cup Winners' Cup Watson would play in the following year.

Playing as centre-forward, Dave failed to score in 13 games prior to the sacking of Brown. Caretaker-manager Billy Elliott played him up front in a home game against Aston Villa, where again he didn't get his name in the paper as a scorer. Next time out at Carlisle, Watson was tried at centre-half and looked like he'd never played there as Sunderland leaked three early goals and lost 4-3. Elliott persevered though and when Bob Stokoe - a cup-winning centre-half with Newcastle - took over, he kept Watson at centre-back, Dave scoring the first goal of Stokoe's reign.

No-one would score more than the four goals Watson scored in the glorious cup run, as Stokoe's Stars sensationally won the FA Cup at Wembley with Watson walking away with the Man of the Match award, despite Jim Montgomery's legendary double save.

WATSON

Watson stayed with Sunderland for another two seasons, before leaving to further his career when Sunderland failed to gain promotion following a last-day defeat at Aston Villa in 1975. Dave was almost 29 when he finally made his top-flight debut with Manchester City.

Born ten years and a day after Charlie Hurley, Watson kept Hurley out of the Sunderland XI picked by veteran journalist Doug Weatherall when he chose his best-ever Sunderland side after 75 years of watching the Lads.

FULL NAME:
David Vernon Watson

POSITION:
Centre-half or centre-forward

DATE OF BIRTH:
5 October 1946

PLACE OF BIRTH:
Stepleford, Notts

SUNDERLAND DEBUT:
Watford 1-1 Sunderland
19 December 1970

APPEARANCES:
212

GOALS:
33

FULL NAME:
William Watson

POSITION:
Right-half

DATE OF BIRTH:
7 March 1920

PLACE OF BIRTH:
Bolton on Dearne, Yorks

SUNDERLAND DEBUT:
Sunderland 3-2 Derby County
31 August 1946

APPEARANCES:
223

GOALS:
16

Only twelve men have ever played for England at football and cricket, with only Arthur Milton of Arsenal and Gloucestershire doing so since Willie Watson.

Watson won four full caps at football, including one at Roker Park against Wales in 1950, a year in which he went to the World Cup as England participated for the first time, although Willie didn't appear in the tournament.

As a cricketer he represented England 23 times, scoring 879 runs for an average of 25.85 with a highest score of 116. Of the other eleven 'double internationals' none made more than Watson's combined total of 27 appearances for his country, a figure Watson may have increased if not for losing six years of his career to World War Two. He also played in two 'Victory' internationals and three 'B' games.

Watson's versatility was also seen on the football pitch. At best as a right-half, he had started as an outside-left before World War Two and could also operate as an inside-left. Watson's pedigree was undoubted. His dad, also Willie, had won the league title three years running as part of Huddersfield's classic side of the twenties, while the Sunderland man's elder brother Albert, was also a professional footballer.

A noted ball-winner, Watson had the ability to use the ball once he'd won it and was a terrific passer. As a cricketer he scored

WILLIE WATSON

over 25,000 runs for Yorkshire and Leicestershire. Multi-talented, he ended his footballing days as player-manager of Halifax Town, then a league side, from 1954 to 1956.

Small wonder that for many years afterwards, sports aficionados in Sunderland would head to Willie Watson's sports shop to buy their equipment.

HA'WAY

the Lads